Readers' Theater, Grade 8: Science and Social Studies Topics

Contents

Introduction

Readers' Theater: Science and Social Studies is a program that provides engaging fluency instruction for all your readers!

Students at different reading levels

- Practice the same selections
- Pursue the same instructional goals
- Interact and build fluency together!

Students build fluency through readers' theater plays on science or social studies topics.

Each play has six character roles at different reading levels (measured by the Flesch-Kincaid readability scale). Use the reading levels as a guide, not a rule. In some instances, the readability levels may be somewhat misleading, as they are determined in part by syllable count. If a multi-syllable word is repeated frequently in a character's role, the role appears to be at a high reading level. Once the student masters the word, that part of the role is no longer as challenging.

The instructional power of the small mixed-ability group is at the heart of this program. Each play and lesson plan has been carefully designed to promote meaningful group interaction. In contrast to independent reading, readers using *Readers' Theater* build skills in a rich environment of peer-to-peer modeling, discussion, and feedback.

The program provides a clear, structured approach to building fluency, vocabulary, and comprehension. The key to developing skills is practice. Each lesson provides that practice through a routine of five instructionally focused rehearsals.

1. The first rehearsal focuses on familiarizing the students with the overall text.

2. The Vocabulary Rehearsal involves students in various activities focusing on vocabulary words. Use the Word Web blackline on page 9 to help students master the vocabulary.

3. The Fluency Rehearsal provides explicit fluency instruction focused on one of the following skill areas:
   - Phrasing Properly
   - Reading with Word Accuracy
   - Using Expression
   - Using Punctuation

4. The Comprehension Rehearsal provides explicit comprehension instruction focused on one of the following skill areas:
   - Asking Questions
   - Building Background
   - Identifying the Main Idea
   - Making Connections
   - Making Inferences
   - Monitoring Comprehension
   - Summarizing
   - Visualizing

5. The Final Rehearsal brings all the elements together.

Following the Final Rehearsal, students will be able to perform the play with great confidence and success. Use the Individual Fluency Record on page 8 to provide students with positive feedback.

Features

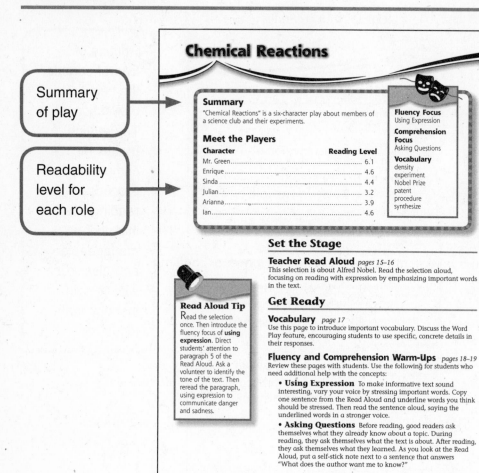

Summary of play

Readability level for each role

Chemical Reactions

Summary
"Chemical Reactions" is a six-character play about members of a science club and their experiments.

Meet the Players

Character	Reading Level
Mr. Green	6.1
Enrique	4.6
Sinda	4.4
Julian	3.2
Arianna	3.9
Ian	4.6

Fluency Focus
Using Expression

Comprehension Focus
Asking Questions

Vocabulary
density
experiment
Nobel Prize
patent
procedure
synthesize

Set the Stage

Teacher Read Aloud *pages 15–16*
This selection is about Alfred Nobel. Read the selection aloud, focusing on reading with expression by emphasizing important words in the text.

Read Aloud Tip
Read the selection once. Then introduce the fluency focus of **using expression**. Direct students' attention to paragraph 5 of the Read Aloud. Ask a volunteer to identify the tone of the text. Then reread the paragraph, using expression to communicate danger and sadness.

Get Ready

Vocabulary *page 17*
Use this page to introduce important vocabulary. Discuss the Word Play feature, encouraging students to use specific, concrete details in their responses.

Fluency and Comprehension Warm-Ups *pages 18–19*
Review these pages with students. Use the following for students who need additional help with the concepts:

• **Using Expression** To make informative text sound interesting, vary your voice by stressing important words. Copy one sentence from the Read Aloud and underline words you think should be stressed. Then read the sentence aloud, saying the underlined words in a stronger voice.

• **Asking Questions** Before reading, good readers ask themselves what they already know about a topic. During reading, they ask themselves what the text is about. After reading, they ask themselves what they learned. As you look at the Read Aloud, put a self-stick note next to a sentence that answers "What does the author want me to know?"

13

Chemical Reactions
Readers' Theater 8, SV 9781419031731

Listing of the lesson's instructional focuses and key vocabulary

Teacher Read Aloud: Use the Read Aloud to introduce the play's topics or themes while modeling good fluency.

Instructional Warm-Ups: Provide focused pre-reading instruction that includes strategies for fluency and comprehension.

Relevant Student Pages

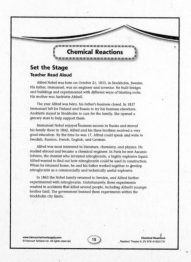

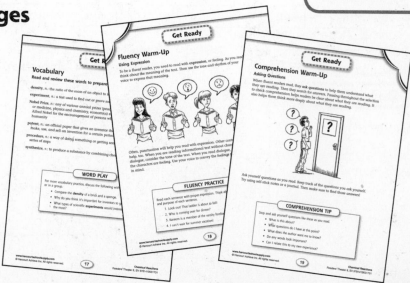

Features, *continued*

Opportunity for students to build confidence before beginning group work

Tip for engaging student groups in another meaningful vocabulary activity

Routine of five rehearsals, the heart of the lesson. The routine breaks the complex process of oral reading down into simple, manageable activities, each with its own instructional focus.

Chemical Reactions *pages 20–29*

Independent Practice
Set up the groups and assign each student a part. Then have students read through their assigned parts once before small group practice begins.

Small Group Practice
Assemble the groups. You may want to use the following rehearsal schedule. Each rehearsal, which should involve a complete oral read-through, has an activity to guide students.

1. **First Rehearsal:** Invite students to scan the entire play to find italicized stage directions. Point out that these directions tell actors how to speak or what to do. Then ask students to read together as a group for the first time.

2. **Vocabulary Rehearsal:** Direct students to locate and list the vocabulary words used in the play. Then have students work together to find and discuss two vocabulary words that are related in some way. For example, students could discuss the idea that an *experiment* is a scientific *procedure*.

3. **Fluency Rehearsal: Using Expression** Before the rehearsal begins, invite students to review the Fluency Tips by alternating reading them aloud. Then encourage students to have fun by overacting— exaggerating characters' feelings.

4. **Comprehension Rehearsal: Asking Questions** After this rehearsal, have students work together to answer this question: What are we supposed to learn from this play? Ask them to list at least three facts they think the writer wanted to teach through the play.

5. **Final Rehearsal:** Observe this rehearsal, focusing on students' expression. For example, when reading Sinda's lines on page 21, does the student use the question mark and exclamation point as clues to reading expressively?

Performance
This is your opportunity to sit back, relax, and enjoy the performance. Encourage students to have fun while performing!

Curtain Call *pages 30–31*
Assign these questions and activities for students to complete either independently or in a group.

Vocabulary Tip
For more vocabulary practice, have students discuss the following:

- What are two fields in which the **Nobel Prize** is awarded?
- Describe the **procedure** for making a cheese sandwich.
- How do you **synthesize** table salt?

14

Chemical Reactions
Readers' Theater 8, SV 9781419031731

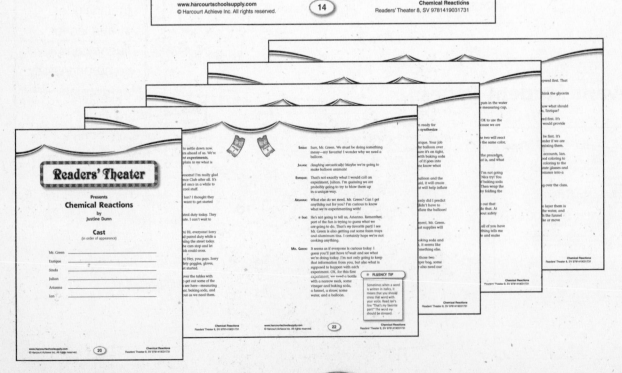

4

Features
Readers' Theater 8, SV 9781419031731

Features, *continued*

Comprehension questions ranging from literal to inferential

Comprehension

Write your answer to each question on the lines below.

1. List the materials that are used in each experiment. Which ones are used more than once? _____

2. What chemical reactions take place while the students are conducting the experiments? _____

3. Why do Ian's gloves turn green? Name another color made by mixing two colors together. _____

4. Why do you think Mr. Green allows Ian to take over the class? _____

5. Why is it important to use safety equipment, such as goggles, when conducting experiments? _____

6. What is the purpose of doing experiments? _____

7. Which experiment did you find most interesting? Why? _____

8. Would you be interested in joining a science club? Why or why not? _____

9. Why is asking questions important when conducting experiments? _____

10. A hypothesis is a sensible guess. Write one hypothesis made by a character in the play. _____

Vocabulary items testing students' understanding, not their ability to identify verbatim definitions

Extension activities for additional interaction, involvement, research, writing, and creativity. Use the blackline masters provided on pages 9–12 to help students complete these extension activities.

Vocabulary

Finish the paragraph by writing a vocabulary term on each line.

synthesize	patent	experiment
procedure	Nobel Prize	density

The doctor spent long hours in her lab. She was working on a(n) (1) _____ to create artificial blood. The (2) _____ was very complicated, and it had dozens of steps. She had to (3) _____ liquids and make sure they were the right (4) _____. But if she was successful, patients who needed blood would have a safe and plentiful supply. The doctor had already applied for a(n) (5) _____ on her work. Someday, she dreamed, she might even win a(n) (6) _____.

Extension

1. Discuss this question in a small group: When conducting an experiment, why is it important to follow the steps in a procedure exactly?
   • Can you substitute materials?
   • Can you skip steps?
   • How might the experiment be affected if you rearranged the steps?

2. What is a fun basic science experiment that you could conduct at home (with adult supervision)?
   • Research science experiments on the Internet.
   • Ask your science teacher for ideas.
   • Create a chart that details your experiment, including safety precautions, materials, procedure, and expected actual results.

Index of Reading Comprehension and Fluency Skills

Correlation to Standards

Unit 1: Science and Health

Chemical Reactions *Pages 13–31*

Science Standards: Understands physical and chemical properties of matter
   Identifies evidence that a chemical reaction has taken place

What's Green and . . . ? *Pages 32–50*

Science Standard: Explains that similarities among organisms are found in external and internal anatomical features

Something Is Mushrooming! *Pages 51–69*

Science Standards: Understands the impact of science and technology on the environment
   Proposes viable methods of responding to an identified need or problem

The Technology Experiment *Pages 70–88*

Science Standard: Compares risks and benefits of technological advances

Unit 2: Social Studies

Cities Around the World *Pages 89–107*

Social Studies Standard: Describes the economic, political, cultural, and social processes that interact to shape patterns of human populations, with emphasis on the demographic structure of a population and reasons for variation between places, including developing and developed nations; the causes and types of human migration and its effect on places; the causes and effects of settlement patterns, including how rural-to-urban migration leads to urbanization; the distributions of cultures and how they create a cultural landscape, both locally and in other parts of the world; and the factors that influence the location, distribution, and interrelationships of economic activities in different regions

The Simple Life *Pages 108–126*

Social Studies Standard: Describes how cultural norms influence different economic activities of men and women in different regions, including literacy, occupations, clothing, and property rights

Individual Fluency Record

	Needs Improvement	Satisfactory	Excellent
Expression			
Uses correct intonation for statements			
Uses correct intonation for questions			
Uses correct intonation for commands			
Uses correct intonation for exclamations			
Interjects character's emotions and moods			
Reads words in all capitals to express character's emotions			
Reads words in dark print to express character's emotions			
Reads onomatopoeia words to mimic character			
Volume			
Uses appropriate loudness			
Voice reflects tone of character			
Voice reflects feelings of character			
Accuracy			
Reads words accurately			
Speed			
Reads sentences smoothly with line breaks			
Reads words in short sentences as meaningful units			
Reads phrases and clauses as meaningful units			
Reads rhyming text at a constant speed			
Reads rhythmic text with a constant beat			
Punctuation			
Pauses at the end of sentences			
Pauses at commas that follow introductory phrases			
Pauses at commas in series			
Pauses at commas in clauses			
Pauses at commas after introductory names			
Pauses at ellipses			
Pauses at dashes			
Recognizes that question marks are questions			
Recognizes that exclamation points indicate strong feeling			
General			
Demonstrates confidence			
Feels at ease in front of an audience			
Speaks without being prompted			
Speaks at the appropriate time for the character's part			
Demonstrates the character's personality			
Teacher Comments			

Name _____ Date _____

Blackline Master: Individual Fluency Record
Readers' Theater 8, SV 9781419031731

Word Web

Character Change Story Map

Title _____

Character _____

Character at Beginning	Events that Cause Change	Character at End

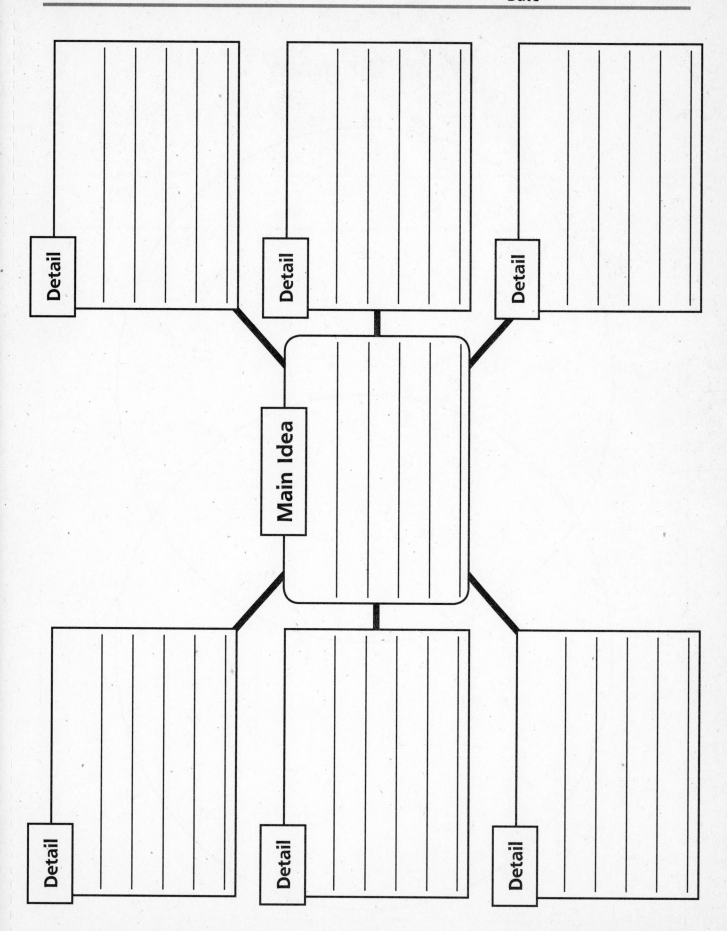

Venn Diagram

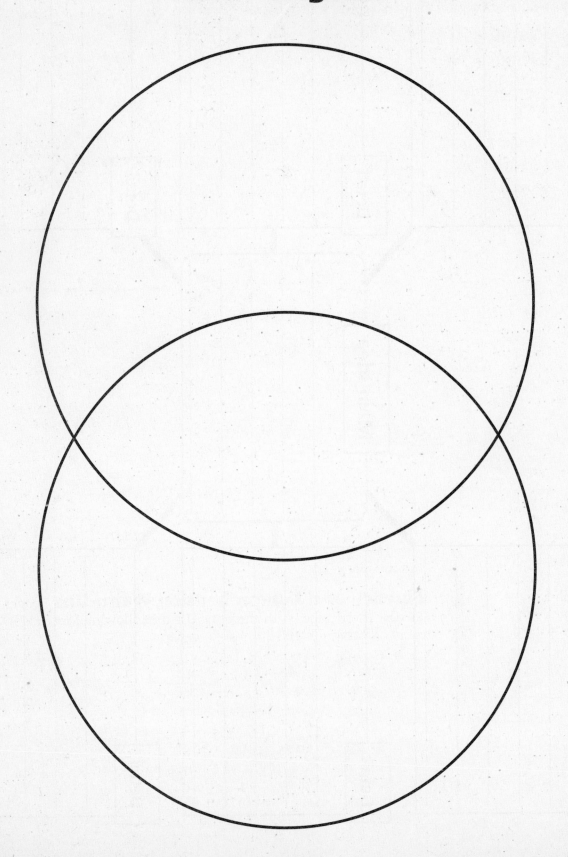

Blackline Master: Venn Diagram
Readers' Theater 8, SV 9781419031731

Chemical Reactions

Summary

"Chemical Reactions" is a six-character play about members of a science club and their experiments.

Meet the Players

Character	Reading Level
Mr. Green	6.1
Enrique	4.6
Sinda	4.4
Julian	3.2
Arianna	3.9
Ian	4.6

Fluency Focus
Using Expression

Comprehension Focus
Asking Questions

Vocabulary
density
experiment
Nobel Prize
patent
procedure
synthesize

Read Aloud Tip

Read the selection once. Then introduce the fluency focus of **using expression**. Direct students' attention to paragraph 5 of the Read Aloud. Ask a volunteer to identify the tone of the text. Then reread the paragraph, using expression to communicate danger and sadness.

Set the Stage

Teacher Read Aloud *pages 15–16*

This selection is about Alfred Nobel. Read the selection aloud, focusing on reading with expression by emphasizing important words in the text.

Get Ready

Vocabulary *page 17*

Use this page to introduce important vocabulary. Discuss the Word Play feature, encouraging students to use specific, concrete details in their responses.

Fluency and Comprehension Warm-Ups *pages 18–19*

Review these pages with students. Use the following for students who need additional help with the concepts:

- **Using Expression** To make informative text sound interesting, vary your voice by stressing important words. Copy one sentence from the Read Aloud and underline words you think should be stressed. Then read the sentence aloud, saying the underlined words in a stronger voice.

- **Asking Questions** Before reading, good readers ask themselves what they already know about a topic. During reading, they ask themselves what the text is about. After reading, they ask themselves what they learned. As you look at the Read Aloud, put a self-stick note next to a sentence that answers "What does the author want me to know?"

Chemical Reactions *pages 20–29*

Independent Practice

Set up the groups and assign each student a part. Then have students read through their assigned parts once before small group practice begins.

Small Group Practice

Assemble the groups. You may want to use the following rehearsal schedule. Each rehearsal, which should involve a complete oral read-through, has an activity to guide students.

1. First Rehearsal: Invite students to scan the entire play to find italicized stage directions. Point out that these directions tell actors how to speak or what to do. Then ask students to read together as a group for the first time.

2. Vocabulary Rehearsal: Direct students to locate and list the vocabulary words used in the play. Then have students work together to find and discuss two vocabulary words that are related in some way. For example, students could discuss the idea that an *experiment* is a scientific *procedure*.

3. Fluency Rehearsal: Using Expression Before the rehearsal begins, invite students to review the Fluency Tips by alternating reading them aloud. Then encourage students to have fun by overacting—exaggerating characters' feelings.

4. Comprehension Rehearsal: Asking Questions After this rehearsal, have students work together to answer this question: What are we supposed to learn from this play? Ask them to list at least three facts they think the writer wanted to teach through the play.

5. Final Rehearsal: Observe this rehearsal, focusing on students' expression. For example, when reading Sinda's lines on page 21, does the student use the question mark and exclamation point as clues to reading expressively?

Performance

This is your opportunity to sit back, relax, and enjoy the performance. Encourage students to have fun while performing!

Curtain Call *pages 30–31*

Assign these questions and activities for students to complete either independently or in a group.

Vocabulary Tip

For more vocabulary practice, have students discuss the following:

- What are two fields in which the **Nobel Prize** is awarded?

- Describe the **procedure** for making a cheese sandwich.

- How do you **synthesize** table salt?

Chemical Reactions

Set the Stage
Teacher Read Aloud

Alfred Nobel was born on October 21, 1833, in Stockholm, Sweden. His father, Immanuel, was an engineer and inventor. He built bridges and buildings and experimented with different ways of blasting rocks. His mother was Andriette Ahlsell.

The year Alfred was born, his father's business closed. In 1837 Immanuel left for Finland and Russia to try his business elsewhere. Andriette stayed in Stockholm to care for the family. She opened a grocery store to help support them.

Immanuel Nobel enjoyed business success in Russia and moved his family there in 1842. Alfred and his three brothers received a very good education. By the time he was 17, Alfred could speak and write in Swedish, Russian, French, English, and German.

Alfred was most interested in literature, chemistry, and physics. He studied abroad and became a chemical engineer. In Paris he met Ascanio Sobrero, the chemist who invented nitroglycerin, a highly explosive liquid. Alfred wanted to find out how nitroglycerin could be used in construction. When he returned home, he and his father worked together to develop nitroglycerin as a commercially and technically useful explosive.

In 1863 the Nobel family returned to Sweden, and Alfred further experimented with nitroglycerin. Unfortunately, these experiments resulted in accidents that killed several people, including Alfred's younger brother Emil. The government banned these experiments within the Stockholm city limits.

Alfred moved his experiments to another location and continued to search for a way to make the production of nitroglycerin safer. He mixed nitroglycerin with a fine sand called *kieselguhr* (KEE zool goor) and formed a paste. This paste could be shaped into rods, which could be inserted into drilling holes. Alfred got a patent on this material in 1867 and decided to call it *dynamite*. He also invented a detonator, or blasting cap, which could be set off by lighting a fuse.

Alfred's inventions helped reduce the cost of construction work, such as drilling tunnels, blasting rocks, and building bridges. He built factories in 90 different places to meet the demands for dynamite and detonating caps. Alfred lived in Paris but traveled to his factories in more than 20 countries. He also experimented in making synthetic rubber, leather, and silk. By the time of his death, he had 355 patents.

Alfred died in Italy on December 10, 1896. In his last will and testament, he designated much of his fortune as prizes to those who have done their best for humanity in the fields of physics, chemistry, physiology or medicine, literature, economics, and peace.

In this play, you will learn about scientists and scientific experiments. Use the vocabulary and warm-ups on the next three pages to help you get ready to read.

The Nobel Medal for Peace

Readers' Theater 8, SV 9781419031731

Vocabulary

Read and review these words to prepare for reading this play.

density, *n*.: the ratio of the mass of an object to its volume

experiment, *n*.: a test used to find out or prove something

Nobel Prize, *n*.: any of various annual prizes (peace, literature, physiology or medicine, physics and chemistry, economics) established by the will of Alfred Nobel for the encouragement of persons who work for the interests of humanity

patent, *n*.: an official paper that gives an inventor the right to be the only one to make, use, and sell an invention for a certain period of time

procedure, *n*.: a way of doing something or getting something done, often by a series of steps

synthesize, *v*.: to produce a substance by combining chemical elements

WORD PLAY

For more vocabulary practice, discuss the following with a partner or in a group.

- Compare the **density** of a brick and a sponge.
- Why do you think it's important for inventors to get **patents**?
- What types of scientific **experiments** would interest you the most?

Fluency Warm-Up

Using Expression

To be a fluent reader, you need to read with **expression**, or feeling. As you read, think about the meaning of the text. Then use the tone and rhythm of your voice to express that meaning.

Often, punctuation will help you read with expression. Other context clues can help, too. When you are reading informational text without characters and dialogue, consider the tone of the text. When you read dialogue, imagine what the characters are feeling. Use your voice to convey the feelings the author had in mind.

FLUENCY PRACTICE

Read each sentence with proper expression. Think about the punctuation and purpose of each sentence.

1. Look out! That ladder is about to fall!

2. Who is coming over for dinner?

3. Kareem is a member of the varsity football team.

4. I can't wait for summer vacation!

Comprehension Warm-Up

Asking Questions

When fluent readers read, they **ask questions** to help them understand what they are reading. Then they search for answers. Pausing throughout the selection to check comprehension helps readers be clear about what they are reading. It also helps them think more deeply about what they are reading.

Ask yourself questions as you read. Keep track of the questions you ask yourself. Try using self-stick notes or a journal. Then make sure to find those answers!

COMPREHENSION TIP

Stop and ask yourself questions like these as you read.

- What is this about?
- What questions do I have at this point?
- What does the author want me to know?
- Do any words look important?
- Can I relate this to my own experience?

Readers' Theater

Presents
Chemical Reactions
by
Justine Dunn

Cast
(in order of appearance)

Mr. Green   _____

Enrique   _____

Sinda   _____

Julian   _____

Arianna   _____

Ian   _____

MR. GREEN: OK, everyone, let's start to settle down now. We have a busy few hours ahead of us. We're going to do three different **experiments**, and you are going to explain *to me* what is happening in each.

ENRIQUE: This is going to be so awesome! I'm really glad I decided to join the Science Club after all. It's worth staying after school once in a while to be able to see all of this cool stuff.

SINDA: Where are Arianna and Ian? I thought they would be here by now. I want to get started on these experiments!

JULIAN: I think they both had patrol duty today. They should be here any minute. I can't wait to get started either.

ARIANNA: *(coming into the classroom)* Hi, everyone! Sorry we're a little late. We had patrol duty while a family of geese was crossing the street today. We had to make all of the cars stop and let them go by before the kids could cross.

IAN: *(coming into the classroom)* Hey, you guys. Sorry we're late. I'll get the safety goggles, gloves, and aprons so we can get started.

MR. GREEN: Sinda, will you please cover the tables with newspaper? I'm going to get out some of the supplies we'll need. Let's see here—measuring cups, some bowls, vinegar, baking soda, and a balloon. I'll get more out as we need them.

Readers' Theater 8, SV 9781419031731

SINDA: Sure, Mr. Green. We must be doing something messy—my favorite! I wonder why we need a balloon.

JULIAN: *(laughing sarcastically)* Maybe we're going to make balloon animals!

ENRIQUE: That's not exactly what I would call an experiment, Julian. I'm guessing we are probably going to try to blow them up in a unique way.

ARIANNA: What else do we need, Mr. Green? Can I get anything out for you? I'm curious to know what we're experimenting with!

✳ **IAN:** He's not going to tell us, Arianna. Remember, part of the fun is trying to guess what we are going to do. That's *my* favorite part! I see Mr. Green is also getting out some foam trays and aluminum tins. I certainly hope we're not cooking anything.

MR. GREEN: It seems as if everyone is curious today. I guess you'll just have to wait and see what we're doing today. I'm not only going to keep that information from you, but also what is supposed to happen with each experiment. OK, for this first experiment, we need a bottle with a narrow neck, some vinegar and baking soda, a funnel, a straw, some water, and a balloon.

✳ **FLUENCY TIP**

Sometimes when a word is written in italics, it means that you should stress that word with your voice. Read Ian's line "That's *my* favorite part!" The word *my* should be stressed.

Chemical Reactions
Readers' Theater 8, SV 9781419031731

JULIAN: Cool! Are we making water balloons? Maybe we can have a water balloon fight outside!

SINDA: *(rolling her eyes)* You boys are impossible! I don't think you'll be winning the **Nobel Prize** for water balloons, Julian.

IAN: I know that when vinegar and baking soda are mixed, they create a fizzing solution. I wonder what that has to do with the balloon.

ENRIQUE: Maybe the fizzy solution will help us inflate the balloon. But what is the straw for? I certainly hope we're not going to drink vinegar.

ARIANNA: Why don't we all pipe down and let Mr. Green tell us the steps of the **procedure**? It's important to follow them exactly as he tells us, or the experiment won't be successful.

MR. GREEN: Maybe you can all take turns performing each step. First, someone needs to pour about an inch of liquid—half vinegar, half water—into the bottle. Use the funnel so you don't spill.

SINDA: I'll take the first step. That way I can watch the rest of you and see what happens.

JULIAN: I'll take the next step, Mr. Green. What should I do now?

MR. GREEN: Julian, you can use the straw to fill the balloon half full of baking soda. Put the straw into the baking soda, put your finger over the top of the straw, and lift it out. Then put the straw into the balloon and gently tap it.

Readers' Theater 8, SV 9781419031731

ENRIQUE: What can I do, Mr. Green? I'm ready for the next step. Are we going to **synthesize** a solution?

MR. GREEN: I guess you could say that, Enrique. Your job is to stretch the open end of the balloon over the neck of the bottle. Make sure it's on tight, and let the part that is filled with baking soda dangle over the edge so none of it goes into the bottle just yet. Does anyone know what we should do next?

ARIANNA: I'll bet that when we lift the balloon and the baking soda falls into the liquid, it will create fizz, just as Ian said. Then that will help inflate the balloon.

IAN: Am I a genius, or what? Not only did I predict what would happen, but we didn't have to actually use our mouths to inflate the balloon! *(The group laughs.)*

SINDA: That was a really cool experiment, Mr. Green. What are we doing next? What supplies will we need?

JULIAN: Now that we know that the baking soda and vinegar mixture creates a fizz, it seems like we could use that fizz to do something else.

MR. GREEN: Actually, we are going to use those two again, along with a small zipper bag, some warm water, and a tissue. We also need our measuring cup.

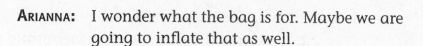

ARIANNA: I wonder what the bag is for. Maybe we are going to inflate that as well.

IAN: Oh, cool! I've actually done this experiment at home before. We need to do it over the sink because it can get a little messy.

ENRIQUE: The messier the better, I always say! I think we'll need more than one tissue to clean it up.

SINDA: I don't think the tissue is for cleaning up. I'm not sure what we'll be doing with it, but tissues aren't the best for cleaning up anything but noses.

JULIAN: Maybe you can lead this experiment, Ian. What should we do first?

ARIANNA: Sure, you can be Mr. Green for this one. Is that OK with you, Mr. Green?

ENRIQUE: As long as Ian doesn't think that means he can take over the club. Remember, I'm president.

MR. GREEN: That sounds fine. Ian, why don't you go ahead and start.

IAN: OK, we need to put one-fourth cup of warm water into the zipper bag. Then we will add one-half cup of vinegar to the water in the bag.

FLUENCY TIP

Sometimes a sentence ends with a period even though it may look like a question. For example, Mr. Green's line, "Ian, why don't you go ahead and start," is a command, so you should read it as a statement.

Readers' Theater 8, SV 9781419031731

Sinda: I'll hold the bag while Julian puts in the water and vinegar. Do you have the measuring cup, Julian?

Julian: Yes, it's right here. I think it's OK to use the same cup for both liquids, because we are not eating them.

Enrique: We are also not afraid that the two will react with each other, and they are the same color, so I think that's fine.

Arianna: I'd like to do the next step in the procedure, Ian. Can you tell me what that is, and what will happen?

Ian: I'll tell you the next step, but I'm not going to tell you what will happen. Nice try! You need to put three teaspoons of baking soda into the middle of the tissue. Then wrap the baking soda up in the tissue by folding the tissue around it.

Arianna: Well, I know enough to figure out that nothing will happen when I do that. At least I don't have to worry about safety for this step.

Sinda: Not necessarily, Arianna. Do all of you have your safety goggles on? Something tells me that the bag is going to inflate and make a real mess!

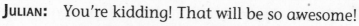

JULIAN: You're kidding! That will be so awesome! I wonder how that will happen.

ENRIQUE: I can't believe that a little baking soda and vinegar can help inflate a balloon *and* a plastic bag.

IAN: OK, I'm going to add the baking soda now. Everyone stand back just a little. I'm going to partially zip the bag closed, but I will leave enough space to add the tissue with the baking soda. I have to do it quickly and then zip the bag completely closed. Then I'm going to put the bag in the sink and step back. *(Ian completes the steps, and the students watch as the bag pops!)*

MR. GREEN: Great job, everyone. You just made a chemical reaction. The baking soda and vinegar eventually mix and create an acid-base reaction. The two chemicals work together to create a gas called carbon dioxide. The gas fills the bag until the bag can't hold it anymore, so it pops.

ALL STUDENTS: That was really fun, Mr. Green. What's next?

MR. GREEN: I love your enthusiasm! Our next experiment will not involve blowing up anything, but I think you'll still enjoy it. First I'd like you to make some predictions. We will be using light corn syrup, glycerin (GLIS er en), water, and vegetable oil. We are going to layer them in a jar, and I'd like to know in which order you think they should be layered.

FLUENCY TIP

Read Julian's lines "You're kidding! That will be so awesome!" Because these statements end with exclamation points and the purpose of them is to show strong feeling, read the lines with excitement in your voice.

Readers' Theater 8, SV 9781419031731

SINDA: I think the water should be layered first. That makes the most sense to me.

ARIANNA: I disagree with you, Sinda. I think the glycerin should be layered first.

JULIAN: To be honest, I don't really know what should be first. Do you have any idea, Enrique?

ENRIQUE: I think the oil should be layered first. It's heavy and thick, so I think it would provide a good base.

IAN: I think the corn syrup should be first. It's actually thicker than oil. I wonder if we are trying to layer these without mixing them.

MR. GREEN: You are exactly right on both accounts, Ian. We are going to add yellow food coloring to the corn syrup and blue food coloring to the water. Let's mix those in separate glasses and use a funnel to pour each substance into a large glass jar to layer them.

IAN: Of course I'm right! I'm taking over the class, remember?

(The group laughs.)

MR. GREEN: The order in which we need to layer them is the corn syrup, the glycerin, the water, and the oil. It is important to wash the funnel each time, and try not to shake or move the jar with the layers.

IAN: I have added yellow food coloring to one-third cup of corn syrup. Now I will pour it through the funnel into the jar. I got some of the food coloring on my gloves, but it will eventually wash off.

ARIANNA: I will add the glycerin next, using the funnel after I wash it. That is so cool the way it layers right on top of the corn syrup!

SINDA: I have added blue food coloring to the water, and I will add that next.

ENRIQUE: Now for the oil, the final layer. It is really amazing that none of these are mixing together.

JULIAN: I didn't know that you could layer liquids like that. Why does that work, Mr. Green?

MR. GREEN: Each liquid has its own **density** (DEN si tee), or the amount of something per unit of area or volume. You added the liquids in order from highest to lowest density. The oil stays on top because it is the least dense.

IAN: Oh, no! I was putting the cap on the blue food coloring and some of it spilled onto my gloves, too!

ARIANNA: Now you really *can* be Mr. Green! Maybe you can get a **patent** on that color!

(The group laughs.)

Comprehension

Write your answer to each question on the lines below.

1. List the materials that are used in each experiment. Which ones are used more than once? _____

   _____

2. What chemical reactions take place while the students are conducting the experiments? _____

   _____

3. Why do Ian's gloves turn green? Name another color made by mixing two colors together. _____

   _____

4. Why do you think Mr. Green allows Ian to take over the class? _____

   _____

5. Why is it important to use safety equipment, such as goggles, when conducting experiments? _____

   _____

6. What is the purpose of doing experiments? _____

   _____

7. Which experiment did you find most interesting? Why? _____

   _____

   _____

8. Would you be interested in joining a science club? Why or why not? _____

   _____

9. Why is asking questions important when conducting experiments? _____

   _____

10. A hypothesis is a sensible guess. Write one hypothesis made by a character in the play. _____

   _____

Vocabulary

Finish the paragraph by writing a vocabulary term on each line.

> synthesize   patent   experiment
> procedure   Nobel Prize   density

The doctor spent long hours in her lab. She was working on

a(n) (1) _____ to create artificial blood. The

(2) _____ was very complicated, and it had dozens

of steps. She had to (3) _____ liquids and make sure

they were the right (4) _____. But if she was successful,

patients who needed blood would have a safe and plentiful supply. The doctor

had already applied for a(n) (5) _____ on her work.

Someday, she dreamed, she might even win a(n) (6) _____.

Extension

1. Discuss this question in a small group: When conducting an experiment, why is it important to follow the steps in a procedure exactly?

   - Can you substitute materials?

   - Can you skip steps?

   - How might the experiment be affected if you rearranged the steps?

2. What is a fun basic science experiment that you could conduct at home (with adult supervision)?

   - Research science experiments on the Internet.

   - Ask your science teacher for ideas.

   - Create a chart that details your experiment, including safety precautions, materials, procedure, and expected actual results.

What's Green and . . . ?

Summary

"What's Green and . . . ?" is a six-character play about students who are dissecting frogs.

Meet the Players

Character	Reading Level
Mr. Carver	6.5
Zoey	4.6
Jordan	4.9
Antonio	7.2
Liu	6.8
Cary	4.5

Fluency Focus
Using Punctuation

Comprehension Focus
Building Background

Vocabulary
anatomy
cavity
chambers
circulatory system
digestive system
dissection
nervous system

Set the Stage

Teacher Read Aloud *pages 34–35*
This selection is about skin and the way it protects the body. Read the selection aloud, focusing on pausing when you reach commas or dashes and stopping at periods.

Get Ready

Vocabulary *page 36*
Use this page to introduce important vocabulary. Discuss the Word Play feature, reminding students to use the supplied definitions to help with their responses.

Fluency and Comprehension Warm-Ups *pages 37–38*
Review these pages with students. Use the following for students who need additional help with the concepts:

- **Using Punctuation** Paying attention to punctuation helps you know how to read a selection. Always remember to pause when you come to a comma. A colon or dash means a slightly longer pause. Study paragraph 2 of the Read Aloud to find commas, dashes, and a colon. Read the paragraph aloud, using the punctuation as a guide.

- **Building Background** Thinking about what you already know about a topic helps you understand what you read. List five things you already know about your skin. Underline one fact that helps you understand what the Read Aloud is about.

Read Aloud Tip

Introduce the fluency focus of **using punctuation** by reviewing the function of commas, periods, dashes, colons, question marks, and exclamation points. Direct students' attention to paragraph 1 of the Read Aloud. Have them identify the punctuation marks used. Then ask them to read the paragraph in unison, using the punctuation as a guide.

What's Green and . . . ? *pages 39–48*

Independent Practice
Set up the groups and assign each student a part. Then have students read through their assigned parts once before small group practice begins.

Small Group Practice
Assemble the groups. You may want to use the following rehearsal schedule. Each rehearsal, which should involve a complete oral read-through, has an activity to guide students.

1. First Rehearsal: Invite students to read the title and list of characters and to scan the text of the play. Ask volunteers to predict what happens to the characters. Then have students read together as a group for the first time.

2. Vocabulary Rehearsal: Have students locate the vocabulary words *circulatory system*, *digestive system*, and *nervous system* used in the play. Then have each group choose one body system to describe in the form of a Word Web. Provide time for groups to share their Word Webs. Use the Word Web on page 9.

3. Fluency Rehearsal: Using Punctuation Before this rehearsal, ask students to look through their lines to locate a dash, an ellipsis, or italicized text. Have them practice using the punctuation as a guide while reading the lines. After the rehearsal, ask them to read the same lines aloud in their groups.

4. Comprehension Rehearsal: Building Background Before this rehearsal, have students brainstorm a list of things they already know about human body systems. After the rehearsal, have groups refer to the list and underline information that applies to both the human body and a frog's body.

5. Final Rehearsal: Observe this rehearsal, focusing on students' attention to punctuation. For example, on page 44, does the student reading Jordan's part say the individual letters in the word *ducts*, as the hyphens indicate?

Performance
This is your opportunity to sit back, relax, and enjoy the performance. Encourage students to have fun while performing!

Curtain Call *pages 49–50*
Assign these questions and activities for students to complete either independently or in a group.

Vocabulary Tip

For more vocabulary practice, have students discuss the following:

- Name two parts of the human **circulatory system**.

- What would you find in the **chambers** of the heart?

- Why do you think some schools require students to do **dissections**?

What's Green and . . . ?

Set the Stage
Teacher Read Aloud

What's the largest organ in your body, is waterproof, repairs itself, and protects all your other organs? Skin, of course! Without skin, your insides would fall outside. You wouldn't be able to touch anything or feel anything. Your body would get too hot or too cold. Germs would fly in, and your bodily fluids would leak out. Pretty special stuff, skin is.

Your skin is made up of three layers: the epidermis, the dermis, and a subcutaneous fatty layer. Let's start by looking at the top layer first—the epidermis—the part of the skin that you can see.

When you look at your epidermis, nothing appears to be happening. It is, however, hard at work. New cells are forming directly under the skin you see. As they grow, they work themselves upward. The older cells die. In actuality, the skin you see when you look at your body is really a layer of dead skin cells. They are strong and tough and provide the protection your body needs, but they eventually flake off and are replaced by the newer skin cells. In fact, we lose 30,000 to 40,000 surface skin cells each and every minute of each and every day. Since it takes about two weeks to a month for the new skin cells to grow, move up, and replace the older ones, you can figure that you'll have grown about 1,000 new skins in your entire lifetime!

The epidermis also contains a substance called melanin. Melanin is what gives the skin its color. The more melanin you have, the darker your skin is. Sitting in the sun causes your body to produce more melanin to protect you from getting burned by the sun's ultraviolet rays.

The next layer down is the dermis. This layer contains nerve endings, blood vessels, oil glands, and sweat glands. The nerve endings tell your brain how something feels when you touch it—hot, cold, smooth, rough, scratchy, and so on. The blood vessels in the dermis bring the skin cells oxygen and nutrients and take away waste, keeping the skin cells healthy. The oil glands keep your skin protected, lubricated, and waterproof. Sweat glands produce sweat that comes up through tiny holes, or pores, in your skin.

The bottom layer of your skin is the subcutaneous layer. This layer is made mostly of fat. The fat helps your body stay warm. It also absorbs the shock when you bump into things. And it helps hold your skin to everything underneath it, such as your organs and tissues.

All in all, the skin seems to be a most useful garment. In this play, you will read about an animal body with some similarities to the human body. Use the vocabulary and warm-ups on the next three pages to help you get ready to read.

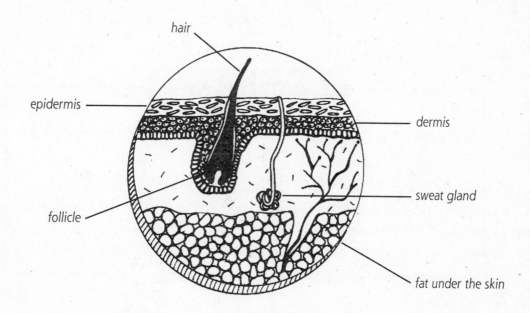

hair

epidermis

dermis

follicle

sweat gland

fat under the skin

Vocabulary

Read and review these vocabulary words to prepare for reading this play.

anatomy, *n*.: the science of the structure of animals and plants

cavity, *n*.: an enclosed area inside the body; a hollow place or hole

chambers, *n*.: enclosed spaces in the body, such as the chambers in the heart

circulatory system, *n*.: a group of related organs or parts responsible for moving blood throughout the body

digestive system, *n*.: a group of related organs or parts responsible for breaking down food and turning it into energy

dissection, *n*.: the process of cutting apart an animal or plant to study its structure

nervous system, *n*.: a group of related organs or parts responsible for receiving sensations

WORD PLAY

For more vocabulary practice, discuss the following with a partner or in a group.

- Who would be more likely to study **anatomy**, a zoologist or a geologist?
- What is a **cavity** in a tooth?
- Is the brain part of the **nervous system**? Explain.

Fluency Warm-Up

Using Punctuation

Fluent readers notice **punctuation** as they read. They know what punctuation means, and they use it to guide their reading. As you read, pay attention to punctuation. Pause at commas. Pause a little longer at dashes. Stop at periods. Change your voice at exclamation marks and question marks. Think about how punctuation affects meaning.

Practice reading aloud to a friend or family member, using the punctuation as a guide. If what you are reading sounds smooth, clear, and understandable to your audience, chances are you've read the punctuation correctly.

FLUENCY PRACTICE

Read aloud the following unpunctuated paragraph. Then rewrite it and add proper punctuation. Finally read it aloud again with the proper stops, pauses, and expression.

Oh goodness she thought as she watched the tiny bear slide down the side of the hill its fur getting tangled in the underbrush He's going to hurt himself unless I do something about it and I mean right now

Comprehension Warm-Up

Building Background

We comprehend better when we know something about what we are reading. Knowing some **background** information helps us make connections between what we are reading and what we already know.

You can build background before you read by looking at the pictures in a book. You can read the dust jacket or back of a book to learn about what's inside. Before you begin reading, pause and think about what you already know about the topic. Think about what you would like to learn and where you could find more information about the topic.

COMPREHENSION TIP

Build background by answering questions like these before you read.

- What pictures and graphics do I see?
- What do I already know about this topic, and what do I want to know?
- Where can I find other information about this topic?

Readers' Theater

Presents

What's Green and . . . ?

by
Judy Kentor Schmauss

Cast
(in order of appearance)

Mr. Carver   _____

Zoey   _____

Jordan   _____

Antonio   _____

Liu   _____

Cary   _____

MR. CARVER: All right, everyone, time to settle down. We have a lot of work to do this afternoon. As we discussed last Wednesday, we will start our **dissections** of the frog in this class period. It is my hope that most of you will also complete them.

ZOEY: Oh, that's SO completely gross! I totally forgot we had to dissect frogs today. I just don't know if I can go through with it. My sister said she threw up the first time she had to slice into her frog.

JORDAN: Come on, Zoey, grow up and get real. This whole dissection thing is no big deal. It's just a little frog. They don't have feelings. They don't think. They don't do anything but catch flies and hang around the water. You can handle it.

ANTONIO: Actually, frogs do a lot more than what you're describing, Jordan. In fact, a frog's **anatomy** is quite like a human's, which is something you'll discover as soon as we begin the dissection process.

LIU: I have an unbelievably heavy load today in my classes, and I'd appreciate it if we could just get on with the dissection. The sooner you stop volleying insults between you, the sooner we can get organized and begin.

MR. CARVER: *(clears throat)* In front of you, you will find the tools you need for the dissection, as well as an illustration of the frog's anatomy. Additionally, you will find some information about each of the parts of the frog that you'll see. I'll be asking questions as you work, so you may want to take notes as you study your frogs. Cary, would you please help me distribute the frogs to everyone?

❋ **CARY:** Sure thing, Mr. C. *(Cary places a frog in front of each student.)* One little froggy for Jordan, and one little froggy for Liu. One little froggy for Antonio. One little froggy for Zoey. Careful there, Zoey, don't eat the whole thing at once!

ZOEY: Oh, gross again, Cary. *(Turns to Mr. Carver.)* Mr. Carver, sir, I don't think I can do this. I think I might get severely ill. Can I do something else instead, like do a paper on frog something-or-other, please?

MR. CARVER: No, Zoey, you certainly cannot. The dissection is a requirement of this biology class. You'll be fine. I assure you that the frog is already quite dead and cannot feel a single thing. This is a tremendous opportunity for all of you. Now, the first step is to lay the frog on its back with its legs outstretched. Use the dissection pins you'll find in your supply box to carefully pin the legs to the dissecting plate.

❋ **FLUENCY TIP**

Cary seems to be something of a teaser. Use the punctuation and the tone and volume of your voice to read Cary's part in a teasing, sing-song way.

Readers' Theater 8, SV 9781419031731

PAGE 3

Zoey: You mean you expect me to stick a pin into its legs and arms? All the way in through the skin and bone and everything else? You've really got to be kidding me. Am I allowed to use tape instead, and tape its little legs and arms down?

Antonio: I know the procedure, Mr. Carver. I recently watched a biologist do this on a public television station special. May I explain how?

Mr. Carver: Sure, Antonio, go for it.

Antonio: After carefully pinning down the frog's arms and legs, make a straight, but not-too-deep, cut from one underarm to the other, across the chest. Then do the same thing where the legs are joined to the frog's middle section. Then, finally, make another cut down the length of the frog's middle.

Mr. Carver: Exactly right, Antonio. Use the dissecting tweezers to peel back the skin on both sides of the center cut, and pin the skin flaps down. Doing this will allow you to look into and examine the chest **cavity** of the frog.

Jordan: The chest cavity is kind of interesting. There's a whole lot of stuff in there. It really reminds me of the insides of a person.

Cary: And just when have you seen the insides of a person, Jordan? Are you telling us that you're a doctor AND a star ballplayer?

JORDAN: No, I'm not a surgeon, and thanks for the compliment about being a star ballplayer! If you must know, I've seen pictures of people's insides before.

LIU: There must be something more you want to enlighten us about, Mr. Carver—a connection to something important to our futures, perhaps? Otherwise, I can think of some of the world's real problems I'd rather dissect.

CARY: Hey, everyone, I've got a joke. A frog called the Psychic Hotline. He was told that he was going to meet a beautiful, young girl who would want to know everything about him. The frog thought that was great and said, "Will I meet her at a party?" The Psychic Hotline woman said, "No, you'll meet her next semester in her biology class!"

MR. CARVER: That was quite amusing, Cary, as always, but I would like to proceed. Let's begin with the **digestive system**. Who can tell me the name of the tube that takes the food from the mouth to the stomach?

ANTONIO: It's the esophagus.

MR. CARVER: That's right. Now please locate the esophagus and the stomach on your frog. You may use the illustration I have handed out for assistance. The food moves from the stomach to the small intestine, where most of the digestion takes place. Could someone name the three organs of the frog's digestive system, also found in a human's digestive system, that help digest food in the small intestine?

Readers' Theater 8, SV 9781419031731

LIU: Fine, I'll play. You're referring to the gallbladder, the liver, and the pancreas. The liver makes a substance called bile, the gallbladder stores the bile, and the pancreas makes another substance called insulin. Both of those substances—bile and insulin—aid in the digestion of what has been consumed. Do you want me to tell you how all the waste material leaves the body?

MR. CARVER: Thank you, Liu, but let's let someone else answer that question. Please take a few minutes, everyone, to identify the parts of the digestive system that Liu just mentioned. They are the gallbladder, the liver, and the pancreas.

ANTONIO: Actually, Liu left out something—the pancreas and the liver are attached to the digestive system by ducts—also like a human's.

CARY: Ducks?

JORDAN: No, Cary, ducts—d-u-c-t-s. They're like hollow little tubes that attach one part of the anatomy to another. The liquids in your body that need to go from one organ to another go through the ducts.

ANTONIO: This is undeniably awesome! I believe I've found one of this amphibian's digestive ducts, Mr. Carver! Is that even possible?

❋ FLUENCY TIP

Liu's speech at the top of this page is quite long. Remember to use the punctuation to help yourself read smoothly and expressively.

PAGE 6

MR. CARVER: It's possible, even though they are sometimes hard to see. You might have to move the pancreas or liver slightly out of the way with your dissecting tweezers.

ZOEY: Oh, would you please stop talking about that? My stomach is doing flip-flops all over the place. It's beginning to feel like it does when I get on a roller coaster. I only feel like that when I'm about to—

JORDAN: Do you want something that might make your flip-flopping stomach feel better? I have a package of butterscotch cookies and a salami sandwich that I've been munching on that might do the trick. I'll share them with you if you believe it will help.

ZOEY: Food? Now? Are you completely off your rocker? Thanks anyway, Jordan, but there is no way I could possibly eat anything AND do this at the same time.

CARY: Hey, that reminds me of another joke. Listen to this: One frog asks another frog who is sitting next to him, "Are you sick?" The other frog replies, "No, why are you always asking me that?" The first frog says, "Because you always look so green!"

LIU: PLEASE can we get on with this? I'm BEGGING you!

MR. CARVER: Now, students, the next thing we're going to do is examine the frog's **circulatory system**. I want you to locate the frog's heart. Who can tell me how many **chambers** a human heart has?

PAGE 7

ANTONIO: Four. The human heart has four: the right and left atrium and the right and left ventricle.

CARY: My mom works in an office building, and there's an atrium in there. It's on the right, but I suppose it could be on the left. After all, it's just a garden that's inside a building.

MR. CARVER: That is quite enough, Cary. You were correct, Antonio. Zoey, can you tell me how many chambers there are in a frog's heart?

ZOEY: Um . . . let me see . . . um . . . three! It has three, I believe . . . yes, three. There's only one ventricle in the frog instead of the two we humans have. Oh, my goodness, I think I saw its little, bitty heart move a tiny bit! I'm definitely going to be sick. Do I have to finish doing this gross, disgusting thing to this poor, defenseless, little frog?

MR. CARVER: Relax, Zoey, I'm certain it didn't move. Everyone, please identify on your illustration, and then on the frog, the three chambers of the frog's heart.

JORDAN: Does a frog have red and white blood cells, too, Mr. Carver? I know humans do, but I was wondering if that's another one of the similarities we share with our amphibian friends.

CARY: You left out the blue blood cells, Jordan. Remember, these are American frogs.

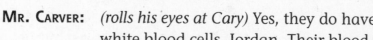

MR. CARVER: *(rolls his eyes at Cary)* Yes, they do have red and white blood cells, Jordan. Their blood is made up of solids and liquids. The liquid blood carries the solid red and white blood cells throughout the frog's body, supplying it where it is needed. Please study the illustration I handed out about the frog's **nervous system**. Again, we can compare the frog's system to a human's. Carefully unpin the frog, turn it over, re-pin it, and slice into its head extremely gently in order to expose the brain. Someone tell me the three parts of a frog's central nervous system.

✳ **ANTONIO:** They're the—

✳ **MR. CARVER:** Antonio, I would like someone else to answer this question. Cary, what about you?

CARY: Moe, Larry, and Curly . . . the Three Musketeers . . . Huey, Dewey, and Louie? Um . . . let's see . . . the spinal cord, the brain, and the nerves? That's right, isn't it? See how brainy I am? Do you get it? Brainy?

JORDAN: *(moaning at Cary's joke)* Somebody save us!

MR. CARVER: I want each of you to study your frogs and your illustrations. Now please tell me something about the nervous system. It can be either something you read or something you observed.

ZOEY: A frog has a really small cerebellum. That's the part of the brain that controls— or controlled, in this case— the frog's muscles.

✳ **FLUENCY TIP**

The dash in Antonio's line indicates that his speech is interrupted, or cut off. Mr. Carver's line should be read just before Antonio finishes saying the word *the*.

What's Green and . . . ?
Readers' Theater 8, SV 9781419031731

PAGE 9

Cary: OK, I can play it straight and participate. The frog has 10 pairs of spinal nerves, but people have 30 pairs.

Mr. Carver: Good, keep going.

Antonio: A frog has fixed eyelids, meaning a frog can't blink. When a frog wants to close its eyes, it draws its eyes into the eye sockets, and a thin, transparent membrane closes over the eyes.

Liu: Frogs don't have external ears, but they DO have ears. You just can't see them like you see a person's ears, but they're there.

Jordan: Frogs don't have a nose like ours, either. They have two small holes that make up their nostrils. The part of their brain that senses smell is toward the front and is called the olfactory lobe.

Zoey: Are we finished cutting up these poor frogs yet, Mr. Carver? I just can't take this dissecting stuff anymore! There's no way I'm going to be able to look directly at a frog again—ever! I need a pass to the nurse's office, Mr. Carver. Please? I'm begging you!

Mr. Carver: You've all done really well today and completed as much as I wanted to accomplish. Please unpin your frog and dispose of it in this bin. Put all the tools up here on the table, and make sure you take home your illustrations and whatever notes you made to study. There will be a test on frog anatomy tomorrow. Have a good day, future biologists!

www.harcourtschoolsupply.com
48
What's Green and . . . ?
Readers' Theater 8, SV 9781419031731

Comprehension

Write your answer to each question on the lines below.

1. What is the purpose of dissecting frogs in school? _____
   _____

2. What are three parts of the frog's digestive system? _____
   _____

3. Name three ways a frog's internal anatomy is similar to a human's anatomy.
   _____
   _____

4. Name two ways a frog's anatomy differs from a human's. _____
   _____

5. Which student reacts to the dissection as you think you might? Explain your answer.
   _____
   _____

6. Why does Liu seem to find Cary annoying? _____
   _____

7. If a frog is injured, do you think it will bleed? Why or why not?
   _____
   _____

8. How else might you learn about the anatomy of frogs?
   _____

9. What are three new pieces of information you learned about frog or human
   anatomy? _____
   _____

10. Do you think students should be required to dissect animals? Why or why not?
    _____
    _____

Name _____   Date _____

Vocabulary

Write the number of a vocabulary term on the line before its meaning.

1. cavity

2. anatomy

3. digestive system

4. chambers

5. nervous system

6. circulatory system

7. dissection

_____ Cutting apart and studying an animal or a plant

_____ Hole

_____ System responsible for turning food into energy

_____ System that includes the heart

_____ Science of the structure of living things

_____ Enclosed spaces

_____ System that includes the nerves and brain

Extension

1. With a small group, discuss how the study of anatomy benefits people and animals.

   • Name three professions that require a sophisticated knowledge of human or animal anatomy.

   • Name two ways technology can enhance our knowledge of bodily structures and functions.

2. In a small group, choose one of the above body systems and research a disease that attacks that system.

   • How does the disease enter the body?

   • What are the effects of the disease?

   • How is the disease treated?

   • Is there a cure for the disease?

What's Green and . . . ?
Readers' Theater 8, SV 9781419031731

Something Is Mushrooming!

Summary

"Something Is Mushrooming!" is a six-character play about a boy and his mom who teach their neighbors about environmental issues.

Meet the Players

Character	Reading Level
Rob	5.9
Mom	5.2
Narrator	5.1
Jimmy	4.3
Lina	5.1
Miss Ching	3.7

Fluency Focus
Reading with
Word Accuracy

Comprehension Focus
Visualizing

Vocabulary
emission
environmentalist
greenhouse gas
humus
nonpoint-source
    pollution
vermicomposting

Read Aloud Tip

Use the Read Aloud to introduce the fluency focus of **reading with word accuracy**. Ask volunteers to skim the Read Aloud and suggest five words that are unfamiliar or difficult. Write the words on the board. Then have students locate the words in a dictionary. Ask for volunteers to read the definitions and allow time for students to discuss the words' meanings.

Set the Stage

Teacher Read Aloud *pages 53–54*
This selection is about deforestation and the problems it causes. Read the selection aloud, focusing on pronouncing each word accurately.

Get Ready

Vocabulary *page 55*
Use this page to introduce vocabulary. Discuss the Word Play feature, reminding students to use the supplied definitions to help with their responses.

Fluency and Comprehension Warm-Ups *pages 56–57*
Review these pages with students. Use the following for students who need additional help with the concepts:

- **Reading with Word Accuracy** When you come to a word with many syllables, remember to look for parts of the word that you know. Put the parts together to say a word that makes sense. Then practice saying the word. Try doing this with multi-syllable words from the Read Aloud, such as *environmental* and *deforestation*.

- **Visualizing** Visualizing means creating pictures in your mind as you read. Writers sometimes use comparisons to help you visualize details in a story. Reread paragraph 1 of the Read Aloud. What comparison does the writer use to help you visualize how much rain forest is cleared each second?

www.harcourtschoolsupply.com

© Harcourt Achieve Inc. All rights reserved.

51

Something Is Mushrooming!
Readers' Theater 8, SV 9781419031731

Something Is Mushrooming! *pages 58–67*

Independent Practice

Set up the groups and assign each student a part. Then have students read through their assigned parts once before small group practice begins.

Small Group Practice

Assemble the groups. You may want to use the following rehearsal schedule. Each rehearsal, which should involve a complete oral read-through, has an activity to guide students.

1. First Rehearsal: Students will read together as a group for the first time. Remind them to preview the play for difficult words to practice ahead of time and to reread sentences that don't make sense.

2. Vocabulary Rehearsal: Have students locate the vocabulary words used in the play and write each word on a separate index card. Then have students take turns choosing a card, reading the word aloud, and using the word in a sentence.

3. Fluency Rehearsal: Reading with Word Accuracy Before this rehearsal, review the fluency instruction on page 56. Then ask students to preview their lines and list five unfamiliar or difficult words. Have them read their words aloud as group members check for accuracy.

4. Comprehension Rehearsal: Visualizing After this rehearsal, have a volunteer reread Rob's description of his compost pile on page 60. Ask students to use the description as a basis for visualizing and then drawing the compost pile.

5. Final Rehearsal: Observe this rehearsal, focusing on students' ability to read with word accuracy. For example, when reading Lina's lines on page 61, does the student correctly pronounce numbers and number words?

Performance

This is your opportunity to sit back, relax, and enjoy the performance. Encourage students to have fun while performing!

Curtain Call *pages 68–69*

Assign these questions and activities for students to complete either independently or in a group. Provide students with the Character Change Story Map on page 10.

Vocabulary Tip

For more vocabulary practice, have students discuss the following:

- Why do some states test car **emissions**?

- Why do you think **greenhouse gas** received its name?

- Can **vermicomposting** cut down on the amount of trash a family produces?

www.harcourtschoolsupply.com

52

Something Is Mushrooming!
Readers' Theater 8, SV 9781419031731

Something Is Mushrooming!

Set the Stage
Teacher Read Aloud

Understanding Earth's environmental problems is not simple. Exploring one problem often leads to finding many other problems. This is the case with the destruction of rain forests—the cutting and burning of moist forests that long ago completely covered all tropical lands in Latin America, Africa, and Asia. Today, rain-forest areas the size of one to two football fields are cleared each second. Only about one-third of the original, huge forest areas remain, and ninety-five percent of the forests could be gone in fifty years.

Why is this deforestation happening? Many people and businesses want the timber, or wood, for construction materials and thousands of other wood products that they can sell around the world. Others need the wood for wood-burning stoves or outdoor fires. Some people want the land for farming and ranching. However, people are removing trees faster than nature can replenish them.

When rain forests are cleared, nature changes. With no trees and plants, soil is washed or blown away during erosion by rains, rivers, and wind.

www.harcourtschoolsupply.com

53

Something Is Mushrooming!
Readers' Theater 8, SV 9781419031731

Some animal and plant species are dying out because of deforestation. In fact, more and more animal species living in rain forests are losing their homes and food sources—some to the point of extinction. Some plant species are disappearing before people can discover them or learn how they might have helpful uses. Many modern medicines for people around the world, including cancer-fighting drugs, have ingredients from plants found only in rain forests. So what happens if the plants are destroyed?

The loss of billions of trees affects air quality and climate. Trees produce oxygen and clean the air by taking in carbon dioxide. With too much carbon dioxide and other greenhouse gases in the air, Earth's climate is warming, causing flooding in some areas, drought in others, and habitat loss.

www.harcourtschoolsupply.com

54

Something Is Mushrooming!
Readers' Theater 8, SV 9781419031731

Vocabulary

Read and review these words to prepare for reading the play.

emission, *n.*: something given off or sent out, especially a gas from burning or manufacturing

environmentalist, *n.*: a person who helps improve problems caused by pollution of air, water, and land and depletion of natural resources

greenhouse gas, *n.*: one of several gases that trap heat around Earth by letting more of the sun's energy through

humus, *n.*: a dark soil substance formed from decayed organic material

nonpoint-source pollution, *n.*: dirtying caused by something started in another place

vermicomposting (VER muh KAHM pohs ting), *n.*: a system in which worms eat food scraps and produce natural fertilizer

WORD PLAY

For more vocabulary practice, discuss the following with a partner or in a group.

- Is **humus** good for plants? Why or why not?
- What are two things an **environmentalist** might do?
- How can a paint spill next to a house become **nonpoint-source pollution** in a river?

Readers' Theater 8, SV 9781419031731

Fluency Warm-Up

Reading with Word Accuracy

Fluent readers read with **word accuracy**. They read each part of a word and blend it smoothly together. They learn how to pronounce difficult words, and they learn what the words mean. They do not skip or add words.

Remember to read each word and think about whether your reading makes sense. Look for a prefix and a root word. Sometimes they will help you figure out a word's meaning. Use a dictionary to learn about words you can't figure out on your own.

FLUENCY PRACTICE

Often you can find familiar word parts in difficult words. This will help you decode the word accurately. Read the following sentences. Find the familiar word or words within the bold vocabulary words.

1. When she discussed **nonpoint-source pollution**, she raised some very good *points*.

2. We *compost* vegetation for our garden. I've got some worms that I'll use for **vermicomposting**.

Comprehension Warm-Up

Visualizing

Visualizing means using the words you read or hear to paint pictures in your mind. The pictures help you imagine yourself in the middle of a story's action or really close to something in nonfiction. Visualizing helps you understand the characters, events, and facts.

As you begin reading, use what you already know about the world to start a picture in your mind. Add details to the picture and change it as you read.

COMPREHENSION TIP

Visualize when you read by asking yourself the following questions.

- What would I see, hear, feel, and smell in this setting?
- Is this like anything that I've seen or read before?
- What is important, new, or different?

Readers' Theater

Presents
Something Is Mushrooming!
by
Jerrill Parham

Cast
(in order of appearance)

Rob _____

Mom _____

Narrator _____

Jimmy _____

Lina _____

Miss Ching _____

www.harcourtschoolsupply.com

58

Something Is Mushrooming!
Readers' Theater 8, SV 9781419031731

ROB: This should be handy—right, Mom? When the recycling sacks here in the kitchen closet are full, I'll take them to the garage bins. Then I'll be sure to get them out early to the curb on Thursdays, like the lady said.

MOM: That's great, Rob. I think that this little house and yard are going to suit us very well. We'll start making our changes outside on Saturday since the weather is still pleasant this time of year.

NARRATOR: Rob and his mom have just moved in. The first week, they started school and a new job. On Saturday, two teens cross an empty lot. They notice Rob. He is busy in his backyard.

JIMMY: Hey, there's the new guy at school. He's made something that looks like a fenced pen, but it's not very high. Do you suppose that he has a teeny-tiny dog or something?

LINA: I doubt it. Look, he's dumped old leaves in the pen. And why is he sprinkling the pile with water from a garden hose?

JIMMY: Well, this is a mystery that I have to solve. Come on, Lina. Let's go. —Hi! We've seen you at school. Lina lives a couple of houses down the street. I'm Jimmy, and I live next door. What are you doing?

www.harcourtschoolsupply.com

59

Something Is Mushrooming!
Readers' Theater 8, SV 9781419031731

LINA: ✴ He's our Jimmy all right—often with burning questions that can't wait. Just think of us as your welcoming committee. What's your name?

ROB: I'm Rob Cleveland, and I like answering questions. Maybe everybody on Earth should ask more. Jimmy, I'm just helping to keep yard trimmings and foodstuff from being 23 percent of the garbage in landfills. My mom and I compost, so it's time that this gets started.

NARRATOR: Jimmy and Lina look at each other. Rob's answer wasn't what they expected. What's with this guy?

LINA: Have you got anything else in there?

✴ **ROB:** Yes, think of this as a nonedible sandwich. Let's see. In the middle is a green-waste layer of eggshells, coffee grounds, and fruit and vegetable remains. The grass from this area is with them. And twigs, shredded newspaper, and sawdust left in the garage are with the leaves in the brown-waste layers.

JIMMY: Gosh, won't that stuff STINK?

MOM: *(entering nearby, smiling)* It will have a pleasant, earthy smell. Rob will turn the pile to mix it up if it ever starts to smell bad. That is just when it needs more oxygen. But hi, I'm Rob's mother and the other gardener of the family. I've come out to hand Rob my poor houseplant that didn't survive the move. Now, would you two like to have fruit snacks with us?

> ✴ **FLUENCY TIP**
>
> Practice long words, such as *committee* and *nonedible* on this page and *environmentalist* on page 61, until you can read them accurately.

Something Is Mushrooming!
Readers' Theater 8, SV 9781419031731

NARRATOR: Two hours of talking pass before Jimmy and Lina leave.

✻ **LINA:** I like our newest neighbors. Each of them really is an interesting **environmentalist**. I had no idea that in 2003 our U.S. homes, businesses, and institutions produced more than 236 MILLION TONS of solid waste for cities to handle. Imagine—about $4\frac{1}{2}$ pounds of waste PER PERSON, EVERY DAY. That's like 100-pound me producing as much garbage as I weigh about every 22 days! I couldn't even begin to drag that weight to the curb. I guess there should be some changes at my house.

✻ **JIMMY:** *(laughing)* Just listen to you, my changed friend! *(More seriously.)* No kidding, I really like Rob and his mom too, and Rob's composting pile isn't strange after all. I'm going to ask him if I can bring over a thermometer once in a while. It'll be COOL to see when the middle of the pile gets HOT. About 120 to 160 degrees is high heat but just right. I wish that he was still **vermicomposting** with red wiggler worms. I'd like to see the little wigglers eating their weight in food scraps every day. Hmmm, *(Pause as if thinking.)* what would my mom and dad think about having a worm composting box in our basement?

LINA: Shall we get my sister to drive us to the mall now? Whoops, maybe not!

✻ **FLUENCY TIP**

Practice pronouncing *vermicomposting*. *Vermi-* comes from the Latin word for "worm."

Something Is Mushrooming!
Readers' Theater 8, SV 9781419031731

JIMMY: Right—we'll walk or ride our bikes the six blocks. Rob's facts about vehicle **emissions** are a little scarier than what I knew. Cars produce a lot of air pollution. But first, shall we go back and ask Rob to join us?

NARRATOR: In another week, the teens are good friends. Rob helps Jimmy research vermicomposting to convince his parents about worms in the basement. Lina helps them set up the new worm box. Mom makes a new friend from down the street, too.

MISS CHING: *(tucking in new plants with Mom)* Seleena, I'm so glad that you've come just in time for fall planting. Maybe I should plant a shrub or two in my yard. Do you have some tips?

✷ MOM: Sure, Mai. The movers probably thought our bags of **humus** were taking up valuable space in the van. But now we have plenty before our new pile produces humus. I'll bring some over when I help you. It will get the shrubs off to a strong start without using fertilizer. Too much chemical fertilizer gets through the ground or through storm drains to lakes, rivers, and drinking-water wells.

MISS CHING: We hear and see that our dear Earth has many problems. It's difficult to know what we can do to solve them. *(As Rob, Lina, and Jimmy enter.)* Oh, hi, kids!

> **✷ FLUENCY TIP**
>
> As you read, look at all the syllables in challenging words, such as *fer-ti-li-zer*, and then blend the syllables together to read smoothly.

Something Is Mushrooming!
Readers' Theater 8, SV 9781419031731

ROB: Hello, Miss Ching. I think everybody can help and needs to help. I found out that planting even one or two trees like this helps in different ways. For me, it was a case of "what you don't know can hurt you" when it comes to the environment.

MISS CHING: That sounds true for me, too.

JIMMY: We learned in class that forests help clean the air by taking in carbon dioxide and placing it in the soil. But how can only one tree help very much?

ROB: Any tree fights air pollution by taking in carbon dioxide and sending it through its roots to the soil. But guess what? Scientists just learned that some trees, like our new sweet gum, do it many years faster than evergreens such as pine. There's also more to know about the power of a tree.

LINA: *(smiling)* I bet an amazing fact with numbers is coming.

ROB: *(nodding head yes)* I think so. A tree can turn aside cold winter winds from a building, so less energy is used for heating. In summer, a healthy tree shading the sunny side of a building can cool as much as TEN room-sized air conditioners running twenty hours a day! That really saves energy!

MISS CHING: That's quite a fact, all right. I do love looking at trees and the birds they bring to yards.

ROB: Something interesting came from lab research about that, too. When people looked at pictures of landscapes with trees, their blood pressure decreased and their muscles relaxed, showing that they had less stress. That happened in just five minutes.

MISS CHING: OK, you've convinced me! Would you all like to help me plant TREES next Saturday? And Rob, I think other neighbors might like to know what you've learned.

NARRATOR: Soon Lina and Jimmy have planted new trees in their yards. Kids from the neighborhood pull their parents into Rob's yard one day. It's the day that Uncle Tyrone helps put solar panels on the roof. Rob carefully answers the kids' questions about how the simple system works. It will power the new water heater and porch lights.

MOM: This system will help me save money, of course. It also helps me feel better about doing more for Earth. Why, we people in the United States use almost thirty percent of the world's energy! We will run out of the old kinds of energy someday, and we produce far more **greenhouse gases** than any other nation on the planet. How sad is that?

MISS CHING: Seleena has shown me something fun to do. Parents, may I invite you and your kids over for a solar cooking day? We'll fold cardboard and cover it with aluminum foil to make a meal for all of us.

LINA AND JIMMY: Please, Miss Ching. May we come, too?

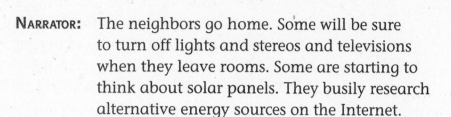

NARRATOR: The neighbors go home. Some will be sure to turn off lights and stereos and televisions when they leave rooms. Some are starting to think about solar panels. They busily research alternative energy sources on the Internet.

ROB: Mom, I'm noticing that everybody is curious about us. Then we share our thoughts, and people want to do something.

MOM: *(grinning)* I've noticed that, too. Something is mushrooming, and I think that's good!

NARRATOR: One day, Rob and Mom finally meet the man who owns the empty lot behind their home. Mr. Peters stops jogging. He just can't keep from asking about these people using huge hammers. Why are they breaking up a perfectly fine concrete walkway leading to their front door?

MOM: We'll lay small stones and bricks that will let rain and melting snow soak into the ground. Do you see how the walkway slopes? We don't want the water to cause erosion or to carry pollution into storm drains.

✳ **ROB:** Stuff from our roof and driveway and materials such as house paint could cause **nonpoint-source pollution** miles away. They could be carried by water to other places, like drinking supplies and rivers. Would you like to see how we're recycling this concrete?

> ✳ **FLUENCY TIP**
>
> Practice reading *nonpoint-source pollution* so you can read it accurately and smoothly.

NARRATOR: Rob gives Mr. Peters a tour of the backyard. Small pieces of cement are placed to keep rainwater and soil on sloping garden beds. Mr. Peters sees rich humus around plants that are looking very healthy. The yard is a nice place to be. Mr. Peters is one more neighbor who goes home thinking. *(Pause.)* A few days later, the three teens dampen the compost pile after school. Mom and Miss Ching sit, enjoying the birds and chatting after work.

LINA: Who would have guessed that Mr. Peters would take down his "Remember, Trespassing Is Illegal!" sign? Now he's actually inviting all the neighbors to use the vacant lot! I guess he really wants some humus.

JIMMY: Everybody on the street will be happy to have it because they certainly have been planting a lot of trees and shrubs. Won't a big pen look a little strange back there, though?

ROB: I asked if we could dig composting pits. In fact, we, my friends, will dig three. That way, as one gets filled, neighbors can start filling the next one. After the first pile becomes humus, the others will be ready in turn for everyone to use. We'll avoid running out by filling and using different pits.

MISS CHING: We're all getting better at being environmentalists. I'll spread the word about our neighborhood composting. Seleena, I have an idea. Would you help us start a neighborhood garden? It can be on the other side of the tree from the composting. We can start small this summer and do more next year.

Readers' Theater 8, SV 9781419031731

MOM: That's a terrific idea! *(Smiling to herself.)* Yes, something is definitely mushrooming here!

NARRATOR: On the way home, the three friends notice the new girl in the neighborhood. She is busy in her backyard. She has mysterious tubs, screening in wood frames, and something wet. They don't ask themselves "What's with this girl?" Instead, they introduce themselves and ask what she's doing. And then they grin when she answers. Carla is making really cool paper by recycling bits of old paper, lint, and mashed plant matter.

LINA, JIMMY, AND ROB: Wow! You will REALLY like living here!

ROB: And Carla—about your paper—have you ever heard of a great idea mushrooming?

Readers' Theater 8, SV 9781419031731

Comprehension

Write your answer to each question on the lines below.

1. Name three things Rob composts. _____

_____

2. Name three things that trees contribute to our environment. _____

_____

3. According to Mom, how can you keep a compost pile from stinking? _____

_____

4. What "mushrooms" in the neighborhood? Why? _____

_____

5. Which neighbor do you think changes most in the story? How? _____

_____

6. Lina says there should be some changes about garbage at her house. What do you

   think Lina will suggest to her family? _____

_____

7. Which character seems the most similar to you? How are you and this character

   similar? _____

_____

8. What would you think and do if you moved into the neighborhood?

_____

9. Do you think that there are many real neighborhoods like Rob's? Why or why not?

_____

10. List two things you learned from the play that will help you become more

    responsible for the environment. _____

_____

Vocabulary

Write each vocabulary term on the line where it belongs.

> environmentalist   nonpoint-source pollution   greenhouse gas
> humus   vermicomposting   emissions

1. The practice of _____ uses worms to get rid of trash.

2. A person who works to save the environment is a(n) _____.

3. Automobile _____ are a substantial source of air pollutants.

4. Seeds planted in _____ will grow faster than seeds planted in sandy soil.

5. Fertilizer runoff from lawns and gardens is one example of _____

   _____.

Extension

1. Discuss this question in a small group: What are the biggest environmental problems on Earth today?

   • What are the top two, and why?

   • What can you do about them?

   • Will they ever be solved—or only controlled?

2. Work with a partner to sketch an Earth-friendly neighborhood. Add captions. Then present your design to the class.

   • Show where things are recycled.

   • Explain how your homes do not harm the Earth.

   • Point out how plants and trees are used.

   • Include your other good ideas!

The Technology Experiment

Summary

"The Technology Experiment" is a six-character play about teens who give up using electronic devices for one week.

Meet the Players

Character	Reading Level
Mr. Washington	8.1
Meredith	5.3
Jamal	4.8
Keisha	8.2
Taylor	5.1
Wang	5.4

Fluency Focus
Using Punctuation

Comprehension Focus
Identifying the Main Idea

Vocabulary
alleviate
enlighten
experiment
honor
lyrics
minimum
pertinent
volunteer

Read Aloud Tip

After reading the selection aloud once, introduce the fluency focus of **using punctuation**. Ask students to study paragraph 2 to note commas and periods. Remind them that these punctuation marks indicate pauses and stops. Reread the paragraph in unison, exaggerating the pause at each comma and the stop at each period.

Set the Stage

Teacher Read Aloud *pages 72–73*
This selection is about the accidental discoveries of penicillin and self-stick notes. Read the selection aloud, focusing on using punctuation as a signal to pause or stop.

Get Ready

Vocabulary *page 74*
Use this page to introduce important vocabulary. Discuss the Word Play feature, encouraging students to be creative in their responses.

Fluency and Comprehension Warm-Ups *pages 75–76*
Review these pages with students. Use the following for students who need additional help with the concepts:

- **Using Punctuation** Ending punctuation gives you clues for reading sentences. Stop when you come to the end of a sentence with a period. Raise your voice when the end of a sentence has a question mark. Practice these techniques as you read paragraph 1 of the Read Aloud.

- **Identifying the Main Idea** The main idea describes what a text is mostly about. An entire selection has a main idea. Often, so does each paragraph within the selection. Look at paragraph 2 of the Read Aloud. What is this paragraph mostly about? Write a sentence that describes the main idea.

The Technology Experiment *pages 77–86*

Independent Practice

Set up the groups and assign each student a part. Then have students read through their assigned parts once before small group practice begins.

Small Group Practice

Assemble the groups. You may want to use the following rehearsal schedule. Each rehearsal, which should involve a complete oral read-through, has an activity to guide students.

1. First Rehearsal: Have students skim the play to locate information about when it takes place. Help them understand that the play begins on Monday and ends on the following Monday. Then ask students to read the play together as a group.

2. Vocabulary Rehearsal: Direct students to locate and list on index cards the vocabulary words used in the play. Have them turn the cards facedown and take turns choosing a card and pantomiming it for other members of the group to guess.

3. Fluency Rehearsal: Using Punctuation Before this rehearsal, have volunteers read aloud the Fluency Tips. Encourage students to keep these tips in mind as they read. After the reading, challenge students to locate one of their lines in which a dash could be substituted for a comma. Have them copy the line using a dash and then read it aloud to the group.

4. Comprehension Rehearsal: Identifying the Main Idea After this rehearsal, have students work in their groups to create Main Idea Webs that list the main idea of the play in the center. Have them add at least six details around the main idea. Allow groups time to share their Main Idea Webs with one another. Use the Main Idea Web on page 11.

5. Final Rehearsal: Observe this rehearsal, focusing on students' attention to punctuation. For example, does the student reading Mr. Washington's first long speech pause at the colon and all commas?

Performance

This is your opportunity to sit back, relax, and enjoy the performance. Encourage students to have fun while performing!

Curtain Call *pages 87–88*

Assign these questions and activities for students to complete either independently or in a group.

Vocabulary Tip

For more vocabulary practice, have students discuss the following:

- Do you think it would be harder to write the music or the **lyrics** of a song? Why?

- What are some ways to **alleviate** stress?

- If you **experiment** with your clothes, what do you do?

The Technology Experiment

Set the Stage
Teacher Read Aloud

What do penicillin and sticky notes have in common? Both are technological innovations partly discovered by accident.

Penicillin is an antibiotic that kills many kinds of bacteria. Many of us have taken it to fight infection. But Alexander Fleming, its inventor, didn't set out to invent penicillin. In the late 1920s, while working as an immunologist at a London hospital, Fleming noticed mold in a bacteria sample he had left in his lab. When he looked closer, he discovered that the mold was inhibiting the bacteria's growth. Further studies demonstrated that the mold prevented the growth of many disease-causing bacteria without harming people. Ernst Boris Chain and Howard Walter Florey built on Fleming's discovery by producing penicillin to help fight infections. Penicillin first received widespread attention when it was used to save lives in World War II.

While some serendipitous discoveries save lives, many—like chocolate chip cookies and ice pops—add to our enjoyment of life in simple ways. For example, when you need to leave a note for someone at home, you may reach for one of those familiar yellow sticky notes. These popular slips of stickable paper were invented by chance. In 1970, Spencer Silver was working in a lab, trying to develop a new type of adhesive, but found that what he made was too weak for his purposes. It stuck to objects but easily pulled off. Silver abandoned the concoction but never threw it out. Four years later, Arthur Fry, another scientist in the same lab, had a problem. When he sang in his church's choir, the markers he used to keep track of his songs kept falling out of the choir book. He remembered Silver's adhesive concoction. Fry painted some of the adhesive on his bookmarks. The markers stayed in place and lifted off easily without damaging the pages of the book. The rest is history. Silver and Fry's invention is now one of the most popular office products available.

In both examples, scientists working on a problem stumbled onto an unexpected discovery and were able to apply their new knowledge to solve another problem.

Technology is the practical application of knowledge. In this play, you will read about technological inventions that have changed our world—you decide if for better or worse. Use the vocabulary and warm-ups on the next three pages to help you get ready to read.

10/19 Reading: Miguel finished reading his book.

10/19 Reading: Amy chose a mystery for independent reading.

Vocabulary

Read and review these vocabulary words to prepare for reading this play. Say each word aloud two times.

alleviate, *v.*: to reduce or decrease

enlighten, *v.*: to give truth and knowledge

experiment, *n.*: a trial or test to see how or if something works

honor, *v.*: to give your word as a guarantee of performance; to show respect

lyrics, *n.*: the words to a song

minimum, *n.*: the least possible amount of something

pertinent, *adj.*: related or connected to something

volunteer, *v.*: to offer to do something, especially without payment
(*n.*: a person who works without getting paid)

WORD PLAY

For more vocabulary practice, discuss the following with a partner or in a group.

- What do crowds sometimes do to **honor** the United States before sporting events?

- To get a good grade in language arts, what is the **minimum** number of minutes you should read per night?

- Where would you like to **volunteer**?

Fluency Warm-Up

Using Punctuation

Fluent readers pay attention to **punctuation** to help themselves understand and remember what they read. Pause at commas. Stop briefly at periods, ellipses, and dashes. When you see a question mark or an exclamation point up ahead, change your voice to match. Paying attention to punctuation will help break up a long sentence into smaller, more understandable parts.

Practice reading aloud to a friend or family member, using the punctuation as a guide. If what you're reading is smooth, clear, and understandable to your audience, chances are that you've incorporated the punctuation correctly.

FLUENCY PRACTICE

Read aloud the following paragraph. Pay attention to punctuation so that you read the paragraph correctly.

I am glad that technology, which has come such a long way in the last fifty years, has given us many products we use every day: television—both HD and cable—microwave ovens, and computers. I especially like the video games that my brother plays constantly. They keep him occupied and out of my hair!

Comprehension Warm-Up

Identifying the Main Idea

As you read, it is important to determine and understand the **main idea** of the selection. A topic is what a selection is all about. The main idea is the writer's most important point about the topic. The writer doesn't usually state the main idea directly. You have to figure it out by studying the details.

While you are reading, look for clues as to what is important. The title is sometimes a clue. Pictures are clues. Bold and italicized type are clues to important words. Use these clues to help find the main idea.

COMPREHENSION TIP

Stop and think about the clues and details as you read. Ask yourself questions like these.

- What is the title?
- What words are bold or italicized?
- What is in the pictures?
- Who are the characters, and what is their purpose in the story?
- Are there ideas repeated throughout?
- What is important to remember?

Readers' Theater

Presents
The Technology Experiment
by
Judy Kentor Schmauss

Cast
(in order of appearance)

Mr. Washington _____

Meredith _____

Jamal _____

Keisha _____

Taylor _____

Wang _____

(Monday morning.)

MR. WASHINGTON: Thank you to my five **volunteers**. We're beginning the **experiment** today. Thanks for coming, everyone. For one week, beginning right now, you MAY NOT use any of the following items: microwave ovens, computers, television sets, DVD or VCR players, telephones, or clock radios. No video games or any music players, such as stereos, MP3 players, or radios. Please read over the information I've handed out.

MEREDITH: What if my mom uses the microwave to cook dinner?

MR. WASHINGTON: You'll have to make something that wasn't cooked or reheated in the microwave.

JAMAL: How are we supposed to wake up in the morning? My folks have already left for work when I get up. I use a clock radio to get me up, set to my favorite station. So if I can't use that, how will I get up?

MR. WASHINGTON: Do you have a suggestion or idea for Jamal that might **alleviate** his concerns?

KEISHA: You can purchase one of those windup alarms at any department store or grocery store. I have an old one that I always use. It makes a tremendous amount of noise when the alarm goes off, and I've never slept through it.

MR. WASHINGTON: Does anyone else have other **pertinent** questions to ask about the experiment? If not, then we're finished, and I wish you the best of luck and want to thank you again for making this commitment. I recommend that you keep a journal of your thoughts and reactions during the week.

(Tuesday morning.)

MR. WASHINGTON: Who would like to start by telling us about their first night without the luxury of their electronic "friends"?

JAMAL: I bought one of those alarm clocks—the windup kind that Keisha recommended. I'm used to getting up to music, so when the windup alarm went off, I couldn't figure out what all that racket was. I started swinging my arms wildly and knocked the thing over. It hit me in the head. I barely made it here on time, and my head hurts.

KEISHA: I dined on cold cereal for breakfast, which I normally despise. I usually heat up waffles in the microwave, but as I approached the freezer, I remembered that you'd forbidden us to use the microwave.

TAYLOR: Things were terrific for me. My mother gets me up every morning and makes me breakfast, so that was no big deal. Today I had pancakes with syrup and lots of butter. They were delicious!

FLUENCY TIP

The dash in Jamal's line sets off an explanatory phrase. Be sure to pause there.

---

www.harcourtschoolsupply.com

79

The Technology Experiment
Readers' Theater 8, SV 9781419031731

WANG: I have an English paper due Friday that is supposed to be a **minimum** of ten pages long! So I sat down at my trusty computer to start working on it. Then, of course, I remembered that I couldn't use it. It took me until almost midnight to write what I needed to. And it's only the first draft!

MR. WASHINGTON: And what about you, Meredith? Can you share details with the rest of us about what your experience was like last night?

MEREDITH: Well, I was kind of bored. And I usually turn on the television in my room to fall asleep, but since I couldn't use the TV, it took me FOREVER to get drowsy and nod off. *(Yawns.)*

MR. WASHINGTON: OK, great start, everyone. Let's see what you have to say in the morning, and we'll decide if there has been any **enlightenment** or change in perspective.

(Wednesday morning.)

WANG: Remember, everyone, that I told you I had an English paper due and that I had started it? Well, I spilled a drink all over it last night as I was working on it and completely ruined it. Since it's not on my computer, I had to start writing the entire paper over again from the beginning. Let me tell you, I am not happy about this whole thing!

The Technology Experiment
Readers' Theater 8, SV 9781419031731

MR. WASHINGTON: Sorry to hear that, Wang. Imagine how students your age did their papers thirty years ago, before computers were common in schools and homes. Remember that many items that you are doing without were invented within the last fifty years—quite a technological leap, I'd say.

TAYLOR: My mom made me breakfast again this morning, but she forgot and used the microwave. I didn't eat. She got mad and said I was wasting food. Then I made my own breakfast, and I was late because of it.

JAMAL: I had to stay in my room last night. My family was watching television all night, and I couldn't. It was a little boring and a little lonely. I wanted to listen to my music, but then I realized I couldn't do that, either. So I read a book instead and did all my homework. It wasn't too bad, I guess, but I'm not really loving this.

KEISHA: My brother was playing video games, and I wanted to watch him, but then I wondered if just watching was cheating, even though I wasn't playing. I figured it was, so I went and read a book, like Jamal said he did. It's a good book, but all I kept thinking about was how I COULDN'T do this and I COULDN'T do that, and that was kind of frustrating.

FLUENCY TIP

Keisha's lines have some long sentences. Use the commas to guide your reading.

The Technology Experiment
Readers' Theater 8, SV 9781419031731

MEREDITH: I really miss my little television. I couldn't get to sleep AGAIN last night. It's too quiet where I live, and I need some noise in the background to help me get to sleep.

MR. WASHINGTON: Well, Meredith, seeing as how it's only Wednesday, and you've got to get through Sunday night, I hope you find a way to get some sleep. We can't have you walking around town like one of those zombies from the movies. I'm looking forward to your reporting in tomorrow, everyone. Have a good day!

(Thursday morning.)

MR. WASHINGTON: Wang, how's your English paper proceeding?

WANG: It's all right, but it's harder to write things by hand than to type them. My fingers go fast on the keyboard. If I try to write fast, I can't read my own writing and I leave out words! But I made sure that I didn't eat or drink anything while I worked!

KEISHA: I would never have predicted that I'd miss playing video games with my oldest brother and hanging out with him, but I really do! I finished the mystery novel I was reading, and I completed all my homework, but I still had time to spare. I never realized how long the evening really is! No wonder people used to go to bed early a long time ago. Now it is no problem for me to get my minimum of nine hours of sleep!

MEREDITH: It only took me an hour to fall asleep, instead of the two it's been taking me. I decided to listen to the birds outside and the other noises. It was actually kind of cool, trying to figure out what was making what noise.

TAYLOR: I told my mom last night not to bother making me breakfast. I said I would do it myself. I kind of liked doing it myself and not bothering her. Especially when she's getting ready for work. I'm not saying I'd do this forever, but it hasn't been too bad.

JAMAL: I've gotten all my homework done every night this week so far. But I find myself singing to myself more and more as the days go on. I really miss my music. I'm not used to doing things without an earphone plugged into my ear!

MR. WASHINGTON: I'm very proud of all of you for volunteering and **honoring** the commitment you made to this experiment, and I'm very satisfied with the results thus far. Remember that the weekend is approaching and you'll have to figure out a way to survive that, too. We'll spend a lot of time on Monday talking about all of this and summing up what we've learned. See you tomorrow!

(Friday morning.)

MR. WASHINGTON: Good morning, everyone. I've decided that I want you to hold on to your comments until Monday morning when we meet again and the experiment is over. Remember that you are supposed to be keeping a journal about your experiences. I'd like you to write about how this has affected you, and whether you will be making any long-term changes. I'd also like to know what you've learned about yourselves—your feelings, aspirations, and responses to the things around you. You might want to share some of what you've written with other volunteers. Have a good weekend, everyone, and I look forward to our talk on Monday.

(Monday morning.)

MR. WASHINGTON: Well, everyone, the experiment is officially over. I understand that each of you has been affected in different ways, and I'd like to have a discussion about that. Who would like to begin?

KEISHA: I would! I really thought I was missing playing video games, and I was, but what I realized was that what I liked about playing them was that I was playing with my brother. We're both really busy and don't get to see each other a lot, but I could always count on his spending time with me if we were playing video games. We actually talked about that and decided that we'd do something together every week, just the two of us, without the video games. That would be extra time together.

MR. WASHINGTON: It sounds like you value the relationship you have with your brother, Keisha, and I'm delighted you two had an opportunity to have such an important realization and discussion. I'm pleased that the experiment provided a means for you to do that. Who else has something he or she would like to share?

JAMAL: One of the reasons I listen to music all the time is because of the **lyrics**. I always thought that someday I'd like to try writing a song myself, but I was always scared to try. The experiment gave me time to try. I've been working on words to a song I've had in my head for a long time. I think I figured out that if I listen less, I can write more.

MR. WASHINGTON: I look forward to seeing your name as the lyric writer of one of my future favorite songs!

MEREDITH: I fell asleep on Friday and through the rest of the weekend without a problem. There's a lot of noise outside. You just have to listen for it. The birds make noise, the bugs make noise, and the wind makes noise. I still like going to sleep to my television, but I learned I don't HAVE to have it anymore. At the beginning of the week when I couldn't watch it, I was a little afraid, thinking that I'd never sleep again, but it all worked out.

FLUENCY TIP

Notice the question marks and exclamation points in Mr. Washington's lines. Use these cues to change your tone of voice as you read.

MR. WASHINGTON: Good for you, Meredith! It sounds like you've learned something valuable about yourself. Sometimes we become so used to doing something one way, we become dependent on it as the only way to get something done. Subsequently, it DOES scare us when we're faced with the idea of having to change it. I'm glad you recognized that and have discovered an alternate solution.

WANG: I got my paper in on time, but I made more mistakes than usual, which I did not like at all. It did force me, however, to go slower and think things out a bit more than I usually do. It takes more time to write something out by hand, so you have to think more slowly, too.

TAYLOR: I was pretty bored. I decided I like having my mother make me breakfast. I think it's mostly because we get to spend time together that way. She works a lot, and breakfast is sort of our time together. I think I use the TV and my video games a lot because I don't like being by myself too much. They make me feel like I've got company. I can't help but wonder something, though. I think that if I participated in more activities with other people, I wouldn't mind the times that I'm alone as much.

MR. WASHINGTON: That's an excellent realization, Taylor. As I said on Thursday, everyone, I'm extremely proud of you for volunteering for this experiment, making the commitment to do it, and honoring it. It sounds to me like you've each learned something enlightening about yourselves. And that's ALWAYS a good thing!

Comprehension

Write your answer to each question on the lines below.

1. Name three technologies that the students agree to give up.

   _____

2. How long does the experiment last? _____

3. Tell what one student does to replace the use of a forbidden technology.

   _____

   _____

4. What do you think is most likely the purpose of the experiment?

   _____

5. Why do you think the experiment involves some, but not all, electronic devices?

   _____

   _____

6. Which student do you think learns the most about himself/herself? Why do you say
   that? _____

   _____

7. Which student do you think has the hardest time carrying out this experiment? Why?

   _____

   _____

8. Would you have volunteered to be part of the experiment? Why or why not?

   _____

9. Which object would be the easiest for you to give up? Why? Which would be the

   most difficult? Why? _____

   _____

10. Do you think it's good or bad to depend on electronic devices, such as television,
    computers, and microwaves? Explain your answer.

    _____

    _____

Vocabulary

Write the vocabulary word that answers each question.

enlighten	volunteer	alleviate	lyrics
minimum	experiment	honor	pertinent

1. Which word means a procedure for testing ideas? _____

2. Which word is the opposite of *maximum*? _____

3. Which word refers to something using words? _____

4. If you freely offer to do something, what do you do? _____

5. What do you call something that is related to something else? _____

Extension

1. With a small group, discuss whether television is good for society or not.

   • What is good about television? What does it deliver?

   • What is not so good about television? Is television harmful?

   • How much television per day is too much?

2. Write about a technology that has not been invented but that you would like to see invented.

   • What need would the invention address?

   • Why is the need important to satisfy?

   • How would your invention work?

Cities Around the World

Summary

"Cities Around the World" is a six-character play about a girl who attends a Spanish language camp in Costa Rica.

Meet the Players

Character	Reading Level
Narrator	7.6
Kate	5.6
Señor Montoya	6.3
Señora Garza	5.4
Iyo	5.9
Simon	6.4

Fluency Focus
Phrasing Properly

Comprehension Focus
Making Inferences

Vocabulary
appropriate
cloud forest
diverse
domestic
intrigued
metropolitan
Ticos

Read Aloud Tip

Explain that the fluency focus of **phrasing properly** involves reading in phrases, or chunks, rather than one word at a time. Point out that in the last sentence in paragraph 2 of the Read Aloud, phrases are separated by commas. Read the sentence twice, first without pausing at the commas, and then modeling using commas as a guide to phrasing.

Set the Stage

Teacher Read Aloud *pages 91–92*

This selection is about the history of New York City. As you read the selection aloud, model using appropriate phrasing by pausing to indicate meaningful chunks of words.

Get Ready

Vocabulary *page 93*

Use this page to introduce important vocabulary. Discuss the Word Play feature, encouraging students to be creative in their responses.

Fluency and Comprehension Warm-Ups *pages 94–95*

Review these pages with students. Use the following for students who need additional help with the concepts:

- **Phrasing Properly** As you read, remember to chunk words into phrases that make sense. For example, in the second sentence of paragraph 3 of the Read Aloud, it makes sense to chunk the words *By 1643—about 500 people—speaking at least 18 different languages—call New Amsterdam home.*

- **Making Inferences** You make an inference when you combine information in the text with what you already know to answer a question. For example, if you are asked why the Dutch governors called the area New Amsterdam, you might recall that Amsterdam is a city in Holland, where the Dutch live. So you can infer that they named this new city for the original Amsterdam.

Cities Around the World *pages 96–105*

Independent Practice

Set up the groups and assign each student a part. Then have students read through their assigned parts once before small group practice begins.

Small Group Practice

Assemble the groups. You may want to use the following rehearsal schedule. Each rehearsal, which should involve a complete oral read-through, has an activity to guide students.

Vocabulary Tip

For more vocabulary practice, have students discuss the following:

- At a concert, what is the **appropriate** way to express your enjoyment?

- What are two things you might see in a **cloud forest**?

- Would a destructive hurricane that destroyed part of a U.S. coastline be a **domestic** disaster or an international one? Why?

1. **First Rehearsal:** Allow students to preview the play, looking for Spanish names and words. Use the pronunciation clues provided to practice reading the words in unison. Then invite students to read together as a group for the first time.

2. **Vocabulary Rehearsal:** Have students locate and list vocabulary words used in the play. Ask them to work in their groups to create a Word Web for the word *Ticos*. Use the Word Web on page 9. Challenge them to complete the Word Web with words and phrases that tell what they learned about Costa Rican language, homes, food, family life, and so on. Provide time for groups to share their Word Webs.

3. **Fluency Rehearsal: Phrasing Properly** Review the fluency instruction on page 94. Ask students to choose one of their lines that includes a comma or dash. Have students read the lines aloud, using the punctuation as a clue to proper phrasing.

4. **Comprehension Rehearsal: Making Inferences** Write the questions below on the board. Ask students to look for clues as they read to help them infer the answers. Then have groups work together to write their responses.
   - What inference can you make about language instruction in schools outside the United States?
   - What information in the text helped you make this inference?

5. **Final Rehearsal:** Observe this rehearsal, focusing on students' phrasing. For example, when reading Señor Montoya's first set of lines on page 98, does the student use the commas as clues to proper phrasing?

Performance

This is your opportunity to sit back, relax, and enjoy the performance. Encourage students to have fun while performing!

Curtain Call *pages 106–107*

Assign these questions and activities for students to complete either independently or in a group.

Cities Around the World

Set the Stage
Teacher Read Aloud

The story of a city begins in 1609, when an Englishman, Henry Hudson, and his crew aboard the *Half Moon* explore a river while on an expedition for the Dutch East India Company. Hudson's logbook and papers detail his finds. In 1621, the Dutch form the Dutch West India Company and send about thirty families to colonize the area three years later.

The Dutch governors call this settlement of farmers, traders, lumbermen, and slaves New Amsterdam. They acquire Manhattan Island from the Wappinger Native Americans with beads, buttons, and trinkets instead of cash. The people have no idea that these little things, worth only about $24 today, bought something that will eventually become gigantic and astonishing.

The Dutch encourage immigrants to come from many countries. By 1643, about 500 people speaking at least 18 different languages call New Amsterdam home. Beginning in 1647, when the settlement has problems, Governor Stuyvesant's discipline restores order. All is usually calm—until 1664.

Britain's Duke of York sends warships to seize the town! Colonists, weary of Stuyvesant's oppressive rule, petition Stuyvesant to surrender so that no one will be killed. People keep their property by promising loyalty to the British king. The British rename the settlement New York. The British rule New York for over 100 years, until colonists declare independence and win the Revolutionary War. Would the original settlers have been surprised that George Washington is inaugurated as President of the United States in New York's old City Hall? New York is the new nation's capital for a short time, and Congress meets there until 1790.

What would the original settlers have seen if they could have witnessed their tiny colony evolve into the nation's largest city and the world's fourth-largest city?

In the 1800s, Manhattan's swamps transform into 2,000 city blocks with streets. The city becomes a transportation center and home for hundreds of thousands of immigrants, who form more neighborhoods filled with their traditions. The state authorizes the city to spend $5,000,000 for 700 acres to create Central Park. Manhattan and four other large neighborhoods enter the twentieth century as one city, soon hosting world fairs, fine arts, and giant businesses. The United Nations meets as Manhattan grows downward with subways, upward with skyscrapers, and outward with landfill.

The story of ever-changing New York City, a major world capital, continues. We can imagine the original settlers awestruck by the size and complexity of modern New York. And we can say, "Just look at what those people started!"

In this play, you will learn about some other interesting cities—cities in the United States and around the world. Use the vocabulary and warm-ups on the next three pages to help you get ready to read.

Vocabulary

Read and review these words to prepare for reading the play.

appropriate, *adj.*: suitable; proper

cloud forest, *n.*: a high, moist forest nearly always covered by clouds

diverse, *adj.*: varied; different

domestic, *adj.*: within and relating to one country

intrigued (in TREEGD), *v.*: interested; fascinated

metropolitan, *adj.*: of, about, or belonging to a large city

Ticos, *n.*: what the people of Costa Rica call themselves

WORD PLAY

For more vocabulary practice, discuss the following with a partner
or in a group.

- What **metropolitan** area do you live near or in?
- What have you read lately that **intrigued** you? Why?
- What is an example of **diverse** opinions?

Readers' Theater 8, SV 9781419031731

Fluency Warm-Up

Phrasing Properly

Do you remember when you began reading and you had to look at each letter to sound out a word? Now you no longer need to read all the letters. You probably know most words by sight. Your next step toward reading fluency is to read in natural chunks, or **phrases**. After all, you speak in phrases, not word-for-word, when you use your normal speaking voice.

Sometimes punctuation can help you phrase correctly. However, sometimes you have to figure out phrasing on your own.

FLUENCY PRACTICE

Rewrite these sentences and put a slash (/) between each natural-sounding phrase.

1. At 46 square miles, the city of Dublin is the largest in Ireland.

2. The U.S. Congress set aside land for our nation's capital in 1790.

3. My great-aunt lives in Venice, an Italian city famous for its beautiful canals.

Comprehension Warm-Up

Making Inferences

Writers don't always tell you everything they want you to understand about a story. Sometimes you have to figure things out from hints in the story. This is called making an **inference**.

While you are reading, think about the hints or clues that the author is giving you. This will help you understand the story.

COMPREHENSION TIP

Make inferences by stopping to figure out answers to questions like these.

- Why does the person do this?
- How does this happen?
- Does this change anything?
- How would I feel in this situation?

Readers' Theater

Presents
Cities Around the World
by
Jerrill Parham

Cast
(in order of appearance)

Narrator _____

Kate _____

Señor Montoya _____

Señora Garza _____

Iyo _____

Simon _____

NARRATOR: Thirteen-year-old Kate Williams is seated on a plane. She is having very mixed thoughts as she takes the longest trip of her life—alone!

KATE: I know that this will be an adventure, which I want. It will be an awesome answer for "What did you do on your summer vacation?" But maybe I'm not ready for this much adventure. I am headed for a country with jungles, and I don't know the language! How will I get along for three whole weeks, so far from home in Chicago?

NARRATOR: Kate tries to get her bearings as she contemplates attending the Spanish language camp and visiting the country of Costa Rica. The previous year has been hectic. School, sports, music lessons, and friends took almost all her time. Then her oldest brother, Mike, left for dangerous military duty near a city at war. They promised to send e-mails as often as possible, so Kate hopes for chances to go online. *(Pause.)* The plane descends.

KATE: Wow! That's San José (sahn hoh-ZAY), the capital city in Costa Rica. It's ringed with gigantic mountains. Can we really land between them and all the buildings?

NARRATOR: The pilot announces that everyone can get a good look at a volcano as the plane circles the city. Finally Kate joins the throng entering the airport. She finds her bags and slowly makes her way through the immigration desks with other people from around the world. She hears Spanish and other languages, but people speak to her in English.

PAGE 1

KATE: OK, so far, so good. Many people are here, but no one is rushing like they do at Chicago's O'Hare Airport. Now where's the promised sign with my name on it? Good! There's my name next to "Iyo Miki" and "Simon Lepage."

SEÑOR MONTOYA: *(holding the name sign)* Hola (OH-la), hello, Kate. I'm León Montoya, your teacher and counselor. Please allow me to introduce you. This is your family, Señora Garza and little Carolina and Raimundo.

NARRATOR: The assembled group is warm and smiling. Señora Garza welcomes Kate with a hug. Kate feels accepted while they wait for two of her classmates to arrive and meet their temporary families. Iyo, a girl from Tokyo, Japan, appears first. She is wearing very trendy clothes and bows to all the adults as she meets them. Simon, a boy from Strasbourg, France, is also about her age. Kate is surprised that everyone else knows English.

SEÑOR MONTOYA: We can talk in English when necessary, but we will all use Spanish as best we can.

NARRATOR: Each student catches a bus with his or her family to ride into one of the nearby smaller cities of **metropolitan** San José. Kate is glad to have Iyo on the same bus. Other passengers smile at the girls and talk pleasantly to the families.

SEÑORA GARZA: Simon will be staying near you. It is easier for his family to take another bus in order to transport his luggage. We live in Heredia (ay RAY dee uh). You two girls will be in the same compound.

KATE: *(quietly to Iyo)* Compound? Does that sound good to you?

IYO: It should be all right. We are with nice people, and we have each other.

NARRATOR: Kate, Iyo—and Simon, a block away—make the same discoveries. Heredia is a colonial city of many old buildings with some low-rise, modern ones sprinkled in. It seems small and relaxed compared to what the teens are used to. A compound is a gated group of homes around a central courtyard. The houses in the Garzas' compound are connected.

SEÑORA GARZA: Here we are. Our dear old city is quieter than downtown, the business center of San José. We enjoy living next to some family and friends in this compound. Our home makes it easy for my children to be with their grandparents while I work at the clinic.

NARRATOR: The girls have seen their rooms and talked with their families about **appropriate** rules. Invited to rest in the courtyard, they sit in the shade, **intrigued** by a shimmering blue butterfly that flutters from flower to flower. Amazingly, it is six inches wide.

SIMON: *(entering)* Hola. We will see **diverse** beauty. I read that Costa Rica has 500,000 kinds of animals. About 300,000 are insects! *(Pointing away.)* That beetle has also found its way into this city.

> **FLUENCY TIP**
>
> Practice phrasing the narrator's lines. Use punctuation (commas, dashes, periods) and prepositions (*of*, *with*, *around*) to help.

KATE: It is as big as my hand! Look! It's taking off like a helicopter, and it sounds like a toy one, too!

IYO: I'm relieved that it's gone. *(Turning to Simon.)* We are surprised to see you, Simon.

SIMON: Tonight we are all having a meal together. Can you smell food being prepared now? The **Ticos** we are staying with are cousins and get together often. They have invited Señor Montoya to join us. I think Ticos spend a lot of time with their families, like we do in Strasbourg.

KATE: I do a lot with my mom and brothers. We don't get to see my other relatives very often. We all live far apart in different cities. The Garzas' home reminds me of our condo in Chicago, though.

IYO: My family celebrates special days together, but our apartment is tiny compared to these homes. Japan's land is so crowded that we must have very small rooms. We slide screens to make spaces change during the day and night.

SIMON: Let's offer to help prepare food inside. Do you see the rain clouds? My family said to expect a shower about the same time every afternoon. This is the rainy season. There is only the rainy season and the dry season.

NARRATOR: Later at night, everyone has thoroughly enjoyed each family's contributions of food: heart-of-palm salad, squash soup, chicken with rice, and tamales in banana leaves. Desserts are fruits and moist coconut cake.

SEÑOR MONTOYA: New friends, I'm curious. How do you compare our city to yours? What **domestic** problems seem the same and different?

KATE: People here are friendly and very polite. Most buildings are smaller here than in Chicago. There we ride in elevated trains, as well as in buses and taxis. The buses here are very clean. I see a litter problem like we have in the United States, though.

SEÑOR MONTOYA: Yes, we are always working on that problem. This area with San José, the Central Valley, is becoming cramped. About half of all Ticos live here, so we see some problems like littering and lack of safety. When you go downtown with me, we will take precautions as we would in any busy metropolitan area.

IYO: Everything here seems different from Tokyo! No inch of space is wasted anywhere there. Twenty-six cities are together in the area. Stores, businesses, and blinking signs crowd together. Almost anything from anywhere in the world can be found. Technology is everywhere, and so are millions of people and cars. We ride the subway and taxis after long waits.

SIMON: We have buildings close together in Strasbourg, too. Many are old but look very different from your old ones. My city has stone buildings in a German style. Dark wood decorates the outsides. Everything here seems lighter and brighter to me.

FLUENCY TIP

Remember to pause at a comma. However, your pause is short if the comma falls near the end of the sentence with only a name or one more word after it, such as *too*, *though*, and *however*.

SEÑORA GARZA: You live in France, next to Germany. Do you travel to other cities and countries often?

SIMON: Yes. My father and I drive and take high-speed trains to many parts of Europe. A German forest is just across our river. We really enjoy hiking. We also get exercise riding our bikes everywhere in Strasbourg.

SEÑORA GARZA: From San José, we can travel by bus to either side of Costa Rica in four or five hours. But we like staying by our families, friends, and nature. We take time to see and enjoy the wonderful things of *pura vida* (POO rah VEE dah), pure life.

SEÑOR MONTOYA: I'm glad that you used those words. It's time that our new friends learn our important description for what they will be feeling here. And now, I think that these friends who are used to extremely bustling lives need some sleep!

NARRATOR: The next morning, after a typical breakfast of rice and beans, the friends begin exploring. Iyo goes with Kate to an Internet café, where Kate e-mails Mike. She reads some of her message aloud.

KATE: Surprise! I am making new friends from THREE countries! Señora Garza told me that her country has domestic police but no military. Please stay safe, Soldier Mike!

Iyo: Now please, Kate, let's look in shops, the market stalls, and the new mall. I'm guessing that I won't find the hottest new fashions here like I would in Tokyo this month.

Narrator: On Sunday, the families go to the cathedral. Afterward, Simon joins in on a soccer game at the city's playing field and then cools off in Central Park. Kate and Iyo's families drive them past the coffee plantations touching Heredia to picnic beside a waterfall in a **cloud forest**. They have plenty of time to watch a truly SLOW sloth in a tree. Leaving the clouds on the way home, they look down on pretty Heredia, the "City of Flowers." *(Pause.)* On Monday morning, language school starts!

Señor Montoya: Every class morning will be filled with Spanish practice, word games, a song, and discussion. We will have adventures in San José many afternoons. Later I will have some surprises for you.

✳ Narrator: The weeks are great! The teens learn more Spanish and feel more relaxed. They see casually dressed businesspeople and other international visitors on San José streets. They chat leisurely in parks, sometimes spotting parrots that seem to be doing the same thing. At the museums, they learn about ancient people, cloud forests, and gold artifacts.

✳ FLUENCY TIP

Read the narrator's line that begins "They chat . . ." Think about the most natural way to phrase the line.

Señora Garza: Kate has told me about her school in Chicago. Iyo and Simon, will you tell us about your city schools?

Iyo: I'm going five and a half days a week to three years of junior high school. I study English and about eleven other subjects each term, but three are P.E. I wear a uniform. Our school day begins with a morning meeting outdoors, during which we stand listening to the principal.

Señora Garza: Then what happens inside?

Iyo: We classmates put on slippers and stay in one room all day. Everyone bows to each teacher. We take turns for room cleaning duty and go to clubs after school. My next club will be video making. I will take a high school entrance exam.

Simon: I will also take an exam. The results will determine the kind of high school that I can attend. Now I am finishing four years of college. College is our name for junior high school. The last two years include studying two foreign languages. We have tons of homework. My father pays for my sports or art and music clubs. They are not at my school.

Narrator: By the third week, Kate has many experiences to tell about in e-mail.

Cities Around the World
Readers' Theater 8, SV 9781419031731

KATE: Dear Mike, Señor Montoya's surprises were field trips and community service. Imagine me watching a volcano shoot gas and lava about every thirty minutes! I can also call monkeys into closer trees. Back in San José, Iyo, Simon, and I are helping Ticos create a little play area. We will each paint a friendship bench with things about our life and city on it. You will be on my bench with me. Watch for my picture postcards with Spanish sentences!

NARRATOR: The end of the third week has come. All three teens want to see their families, but saying good-byes at the airport is terribly difficult for everyone.

SEÑOR MONTOYA: We hope to see you here again. Wherever you go, know that our good wishes for joy are now always with you. Be intrigued, and have *pura vida.*

SEÑORA GARZA: We are your second families—forever!

NARRATOR: Kate reflects on her experience as she sits on the plane. Finally she rereads Mike's latest message.

KATE: "Dear Squirt, I'm imagining you. I'm also imagining me really being on a bench in Costa Rica with you someday. Traveling with your big brother won't be so bad, will it?…"

NARRATOR: Mike's idea seems wonderful! Kate smiles because she believes deep inside that it will come true. Traveling with her brother will DEFINITELY not be bad.

Comprehension

Write your answer to each question on the lines below.

1. At the airport, why does Señor Montoya hold a sign with the teens' names on it?

   _____

2. What are three things Kate worries about on her way to Costa Rica?

   _____

   _____

3. List three things Kate sees in Costa Rica that she would not see in Chicago.

   _____

   _____

4. List three ways that Kate benefits from her trip.

   _____

   _____

5. What do you think the Costa Ricans mean by *pura vida*?

   _____

6. How is the Garzas' compound different from where you live? How is it the same?

   _____

7. Señora Garza says that about half of all Ticos live in the Central Valley. What can you infer about problems of crowding in the rest of the country?

   _____

8. What would you like best about going to school in Japan? What would you dislike?

   _____

9. What would you find challenging if you were going to a foreign language camp?

   _____

10. Would you like to travel as an exchange student? Why or why not? Where would you like to visit? What foreign language would you like to learn?

    _____

    _____

Vocabulary

Write the number of a vocabulary term on the line before its meaning.

1. diverse   _____ Relating to activities within a country

2. metropolitan   _____ Wet, foggy forest located on high land

3. cloud forest   _____ Different

4. Ticos   _____ Proper

5. intrigued   _____ People of Costa Rica

6. appropriate   _____ Relating to a large city

7. domestic   _____ Very interested

Extension

1. Discuss this question in a small group: What do you think about U.S. students staying in a foreign country for a few weeks?

   • What age should they be? Why?

   • What should the students try to learn in the country? Why?

   • How can visiting a foreign country benefit the student? Do you think host families can benefit? Why or why not?

2. Work with a partner to research another city. Write about each topic below. Then read your summary to the class.

   • Why people started the city

   • Important changes, good or bad

   • Special or fun facts to know about the city

The Simple Life

Summary

"The Simple Life" is a six-character play about a girl who spends time living with an Amish family.

Meet the Players

Character	Reading Level
Narrator	8.1
Dad	4.9
Kim	4.1
Sam Jr.	5.6
Ellie	8.6
Rachel	4.8

Fluency Focus
Phrasing Properly

Comprehension Focus
Making Connections

Vocabulary
conform
consumerism
corrupt/corruption
culture
incessantly
philosophy
reproach/reproachable

Read Aloud Tip

Remind students that the fluency focus of **phrasing properly** involves reading in phrases, or chunks, rather than one word at a time. Point out that in the first sentence in the Read Aloud, the quotation marks are a clue that the words *the simple life* form one chunk. Read the sentence twice, first without pausing at the quotation marks, and then modeling how to read the phrase properly.

Set the Stage

Teacher Read Aloud *pages 110–111*
This selection is about living simply. Read the selection aloud, focusing on proper phrasing by pausing at appropriate points within the sentences.

Get Ready

Vocabulary *page 112*
Use this page to introduce important vocabulary. Discuss the Word Play feature, reminding students to use the supplied definitions to help with their responses.

Fluency and Comprehension Warm-Ups *pages 113–114*
Review these pages with students. Use the following for students who need additional help with the concepts:

- **Phrasing Properly** Look at the second sentence in paragraph 4 of the Read Aloud. Listen to one way of phrasing the sentence: *Many people collect—and over-decorate—and stash.* Now listen to a different way of phrasing: *Many people—collect and over-decorate—and stash.* Which phrasing sounds smoother and more natural?

- **Making Connections** You make connections when you think about how what you read relates to your own experiences. Look at paragraph 4 of the Read Aloud. In this paragraph, how does the writer help you make connections?

Readers' Theater 8, SV 9781419031731

The Simple Life *pages 115–124*

Independent Practice
Set up the groups and assign each student a part. Then have students read through their assigned parts once before small group practice begins.

Small Group Practice
Assemble the groups. You may want to use the following rehearsal schedule. Each rehearsal, which should involve a complete oral read-through, has an activity to guide students.

1. First Rehearsal: Invite students to read the title and list of characters in the play. Ask volunteers to predict where the play takes place. Then have students read together as a group for the first time.

2. Vocabulary Rehearsal: Encourage students to locate the vocabulary words in the play. Then challenge each student to compose a sentence that includes two vocabulary words, such as "The Amish *culture* does not encourage *consumerism*." Have students share their sentences with a partner.

3. Fluency Rehearsal: Phrasing Properly Have students review page 113. Then for the rehearsal, designate one student to be the tip reader. At the end of pages 117, 118, and 123, ask the tip reader to read the tip aloud. After the reading, have volunteers choose one tip and model using it for reading a line of the play.

4. Comprehension Rehearsal: Making Connections Ask students to think about connections they can make between this play and their own experiences. Then have them work in groups to complete a Venn diagram that compares and contrasts an Amish school with their own school. Use the blackline master on page 12.

5. Final Rehearsal: Observe this rehearsal, focusing on phrasing properly. For example, when reading Ellie's second lines on page 118, does the student playing Ellie break up the long sentences into meaningful phrases?

Performance
This is your opportunity to sit back, relax, and enjoy the performance. Encourage students to have fun while performing!

Curtain Call *pages 125–126*
Assign these questions and activities for students to complete either independently or in a group.

Vocabulary Tip
For more vocabulary practice, have students discuss the following:

- Would a person who hates to **conform** want to wear a uniform to school?

- Do you think **consumerism** is a problem in our society?

- Do you think **corrupt** people are worthy of your respect? Why or why not?

Readers' Theater 8, SV 9781419031731

The Simple Life

Set the Stage
Teacher Read Aloud

What does "the simple life" really mean? Does it mean giving up telephones and television to sit in a meadow and write poetry about daisies? Maybe that's what it means to some people. But simple living is really much more involved than that.

To live simply is to be fully aware of how you are living your life and then to live the life you choose—a life in harmony with other people and with the environment. Those who voluntarily simplify usually reevaluate their chosen career or job and thoughtfully consider how they should spend their money and their time. They often make changes in their lives so they can spend more time with friends and family. If they have a choice, they may buy local organic produce and recycle to make less of an impact on the environment.

Some people think living simply means giving up material possessions. They believe you must live in poverty and live a life of deprivation. Though some people might choose this path, poverty and deprivation are not required for simple living. Instead, you alone decide what is enough in your life.

For example, you often hear about people simplifying their lives by ridding themselves of clutter. Many people collect and over-decorate and stash. Perhaps you know someone like that—someone with junk drawers filled with odds and ends, or closets that have items no longer worn, or basements, attics, or storage closets filled with items no longer used. Don't feel bad if this hits close to home. Many of us fall into this trap. But in order to live more simply, we might need to reevaluate these stowed items. Perhaps keep the things cherished and used. Give away or discard the rest.

Another way people live more simply is by doing more things for themselves. They may sew their own clothes. They may grow their own food. This is called self-sufficient living because these people choose to live with as little outside help as possible. By doing this, they feel independent and self-reliant. They also feel confident that what they use is grown or produced in a healthy way that doesn't adversely affect the environment.

Many people live simply by cutting back on their consumption. Those who can afford it may still have a nice house, and even a fancy car, but they don't continue to buy products just because they can. They don't have to have the latest model when the one they own works fine. They purchase less because they want less. They spend less of their time acquiring things and more time enjoying relationships and experiences. When people have a healthy relationship with money, they often have more time to enjoy what they have instead of worrying about what they don't have.

In this play, you will read about people who have chosen the simple life. Use the vocabulary and warm-ups on the next three pages to help you get ready to read.

Vocabulary

Read and review these words to prepare for reading the play.

conform, *v.*: to obey generally accepted standards

consumerism, *n.*: the tendency to spend a lot of time buying goods

corrupt, *v.*: to ruin; to make evil or wicked (*n.*: **corruption**)

culture, *n.*: civilization of people at a certain time and place

incessantly, *adv.*: without stopping; constantly

philosophy, *n.*: a set of ideas and beliefs for guiding life or conduct

reproach, *v.*: to blame (*adj.*: **reproachable**)

WORD PLAY

For more vocabulary practice, discuss the following with a partner or in a group.

- What **cultures** have you studied in school?
- Does it bother you when a water faucet drips **incessantly**?
- What is your **philosophy** about at what age kids should be allowed to drive? Explain why you think as you do.

Fluency Warm-Up

Phrasing Properly

Do you remember when you began reading and you had to look at each letter to sound out a word? Now you no longer need to read all the letters. You probably know most words by sight. Your next step toward reading fluency is to read in natural chunks, or **phrases**. Instead of reading each word separately, read a phrase—a few words in a sentence. After all, you speak in phrases, not word-for-word, when you use your normal speaking voice.

There are many times when punctuation will help you phrase correctly. However, sometimes you'll have to figure out phrasing on your own.

FLUENCY PRACTICE

Rewrite these sentences and put a slash between each natural-sounding phrase. For example: **Fluent readers / remember / to look ahead / for words / that go together.**

1. A new baby was born to the Kang family on June 9—a boy.

2. I figure that if I sell some of the things I don't use anymore, I will have enough money to buy that video game I really want.

3. Kendall was concerned about her mother because the walk had been long and hot, and it was not over yet.

Comprehension Warm-Up

Making Connections

Have you ever read a story and thought, "That's happened to me before," or "This reminds me of another story"? If so, you were **making connections**. Good readers connect what they read to their own lives and to other things they have read.

One way to practice making connections is to ask yourself questions as you read. Then you can use what you know to figure out the best answers.

COMPREHENSION TIP

Ask yourself questions like these as you read.

- Does this remind me of something in my life?

- Does this remind me of another story I've read?

- Does this remind me of something I have seen happen in the world?

Readers' Theater

Presents
The Simple Life
by
Laura Layton Strom

Cast
(in order of appearance)

Narrator _____

Dad _____

Kim _____

Sam Jr. _____

Ellie _____

Rachel _____

NARRATOR: Kim, age 14, is sprawled out on the sofa, watching TV. She chomps her gum and blows bubbles toward her brother, narrowly missing him each time. After her mother's third request, Kim finally extracts herself from her worn groove in the sofa and drags herself to the dinner table. The TV is blaring in the kitchen, and the family watches as they gobble their food amidst the tumult of TV noise. Tonight they eat not-quite-thawed lasagna.

DAD: *(sees Kim getting up from the table)* Hey, Kimmy, wait. Before you head off for homework, please help me clear the dishes from the table.

KIM: *(big moan)* Ugh! *(Rolls eyes and then reluctantly and dramatically clears the dishes.)*

DAD: Don't give me that, Kimmy! You've been home for three hours. You've done nothing but stare at the TV and pester your brother.

KIM: *(boldly)* I wouldn't pester him so **incessantly** if I could have a TV in my room! Everyone else has one! Besides, I need a sanctuary away from the little nuisance.

DAD: I don't appreciate your calling your brother a nuisance. Gee, I have some good news to share with you, but you seem so grumpy. *(Pauses and then continues.)* Do you remember your mother's cousin, Susan? Her husband was brought up Amish, but he left the order to marry Susan. Anyway, his sister Ellie is still living in the Amish community of Nappanee, Indiana.

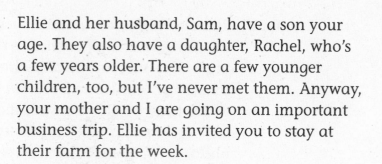

Ellie and her husband, Sam, have a son your age. They also have a daughter, Rachel, who's a few years older. There are a few younger children, too, but I've never met them. Anyway, your mother and I are going on an important business trip. Ellie has invited you to stay at their farm for the week.

KIM: Where is the little fungus going to be?

✳ DAD: Kim! Honestly! YOUR BROTHER is going to his friend Victor's house for the week.

KIM: No way! That's totally unfair! You are deliberately sending me to some pathetic farm, and he gets to have a glorious time with his friend.

DAD: Your mother and I think it would be good for you. You'll learn about another **culture**.

NARRATOR: It's Sunday evening when Kim's dad drops Kim off at Sam and Ellie Yoder's farm in Nappanee. The family embraces her and welcomes her to their home. Kim enters a tranquil scene of an intimate family illuminated by simple kerosene lanterns.

KIM: (whispering to 14-year-old Sam Jr.) So when is the electrician coming to fix the lights?

SAM JR.: Kim, most Amish don't have electricity. Our culture wants to preserve the lifestyle of our forefathers, to maintain self-sufficiency, and to avoid the **corruption** of the outside world.

> ✳ **FLUENCY TIP**
>
> When you see words in all capitals, such as YOUR BROTHER, that is a signal to emphasize those words and phrase those words together.

Readers' Theater 8, SV 9781419031731

ELLIE: Perhaps we should acquaint you a little with the Amish culture. *(Kim nods.)* The Amish are a close-knit society of people who have consciously chosen to live a simple life. We wish to live the way our ancestors did in the 1700s, out of respect for our forefathers' teachings. Our **philosophy** is one of hard work and discipline. We have rules of behavior and custom that all members must obey, or they may be shunned, or banned, from the community. And we dress to **conform** to standards of modesty, rather than to draw attention to ourselves.

RACHEL: About 200,000 Amish live in the United States in about 22 states. But most of the Amish are in Ohio, Pennsylvania, and Indiana.

ELLIE: We rely on our own community for most of our needs and reject **consumerism**. We believe the needs of the group are paramount to individual needs, status, or acquisition of power. We refuse to own cars because car ownership could divide the wealthy from the poor in our community, lead to pride, and disrupt the slower pace we value.

RACHEL: You see, there is more to us than bonnets and buggies!

✳ **SAM JR.:** It is a challenge to live in the world but remain not of it.

KIM: I can't imagine life without a TV, a telephone, the Internet, a dishwasher, an air conditioner . . . !

✳ **FLUENCY TIP**

Phrase long lines in natural-sounding phrases, such as "It is a challenge / to live in the world / but remain not of it."

The Simple Life
Readers' Theater 8, SV 9781419031731

RACHEL: Ah, it's not bad at all, Kim. We wouldn't enjoy television anyway. We would worry that it would corrupt our way of life. We have plenty to do to keep us busy. And when people are sick or in trouble, the community rushes to their aid.

KIM: What about school? *(Talking to Sam Jr.)* My dad said you are in eighth grade, like I am. So do you go to public school, like I do?

SAM JR.: Some Amish go to public school, but we built our own school. The public school tries, but it cannot easily respect our ways and abide by government laws at the same time. I'm in eighth grade, so this is the culmination of my schooling. *(Proudly.)* Next year I will be here full-time, tending the fields and animals with the men.

KIM: Your last year of school is eighth grade! I . . . I . . . don't know what to think about that!

SAM JR.: We arranged for you to come to school with me this week.

ELLIE: Well, we'd better get to sleep, everyone. It is 8:10 already, and the moon is rising!

KIM: You all go to sleep at 8 o'clock?

NARRATOR: The Yoder family easily drifts to silent sleep, but Kim is alert and restless until 12 A.M., when sleep finally enfolds her. In four hours, the rising sun's orange light paints and dilutes the dark blue clouds of morning. At 4:30 A.M., someone pummels abruptly on the bedroom door.

RACHEL: *(brightly enters)* Good morning, sleepyhead. Mother let you sleep an extra thirty minutes. Everyone else is dressed, so please make haste. *(She lays a pale yellow dress and white smock on the bed.)* You can wear one of my dresses, so you won't appear such an outsider.

NARRATOR: Kim dresses and lumbers into the kitchen.

KIM: *(exhausted)* So, what's for breakfast?

SAM JR.: We'll have breakfast later, after we milk the cows. Follow me, and I'll show you how to milk. We have thirty Holsteins now. Later you can fetch the kerosene and help Mother and the girls cook breakfast and pack lunches.

KIM: *(unsure)* O . . . K. You folks sure manage to perform a lot of chores.

ELLIE: For breakfast we'll have scrambled eggs, cornmeal mush, fried potatoes, sausages, and baked apples.

KIM: Wow! I usually just scarf down some oatmeal and chug down a goblet of cranberry juice.

NARRATOR: The children finish their morning chores, eat breakfast, and walk to the Amish schoolhouse. The school is wooden and white and looks like the one-room pioneer schoolhouses pictured in Kim's social studies textbook. Indoors it is painted two shades of a cheerful blue. A middle aisle runs between rows of benches and slanted tables. Each spot has its own slate with a piece of chalk and an eraser. Children's drawings, paintings, and writings adorn the side walls.

Sam Jr.: *(entering classroom with Kim)* We occupy the back because we are the oldest. After we sing a morning song and memorize a Bible verse, Miss Miller makes her way back to us. *(Hands Kim a reader.)*

Kim: *(whispering to Sam Jr.)* Wow! Your school differs so radically from mine. I have eight different teachers in eight different classrooms. We have lockers littered with books—and litter. We rush from class to class like maniacs. When I get home, I usually have three to four hours of homework.

Sam Jr.: *(whispering to Kim)* We never have homework!

Kim: *(whispering)* No way!

Sam Jr.: *(whispering)* Yes, it is our way. We Amish greatly value family time in the evenings.

Narrator: After school, the children walk back to the Yoders' farm.

Rachel: Hello, Kim. I hope school was fine.

Kim: Yes, I adored it actually. It was all really very sane. We had sufficient time to read, and we had a lively religious discussion. And we have no homework!

Ellie: Ah, then you must have boundless energy to assist us with afternoon chores.

Kim: Actually, no. I'm kinda beat. I think I'd like to watch a little . . . oh, yeah.

Rachel: We could really use some help.

Kim: Well, OK.

Readers' Theater 8, SV 9781419031731

(Later that evening.)

ELLIE: Well, Kim, that was an impressive effort for a novice. You beat a rug, folded laundry, scrubbed the floor, made an apple pie from scratch, peeled and mashed potatoes, and set the table—all before supper at 5 o'clock.

KIM: Hope you don't mind if I just droop and wither into this chair at the supper table and rest a spell.

ELLIE: *(brightly, to everyone)* So we have chicken, dumplings, beans, strawberries, zucchini bread, and Kim's own apple pie to pass around the table.

NARRATOR: Kim hardly consumes a morsel because she is so tired from her strenuous day. She is relieved that the young people are not expected to talk during the meal. After supper, she helps clear the dishes and also painstakingly dries each dish, pot, and delicate cup after Rachel washes them by hand. Kim collapses in a heap in the family room.

SAM JR.: We're playing marbles. Kim, you are welcome to play.

RACHEL: We girls are working on our sewing. Do you sew? Would you like to sew a little, too?

The Simple Life
Readers' Theater 8, SV 9781419031731

KIM: I took a home living class last year, and we learned how to patch clothes and to construct an apron.

RACHEL: Excellent. We make aprons and sell them at the general store. You can pick out some fabric from that box. *(To everyone.)* Now it is my turn to tell a story. *(To Kim.)* We make up stories for fun, and it is my turn tonight. *(Back to everyone.)* So, my story is about a young English girl who comes to live with an Amish family . . .

NARRATOR: While Rachel elaborately weaves a story for the girls, Kim becomes keenly aware of the dynamics in the room. The boys play their game without **reproaching** the others. The girls listen intently to their sister's intriguing story. They don't interrupt or fidget. At 8:00 P.M., Ellie proclaims it bedtime, and each child respects the routine and responds immediately.

ALL: Good night.

✳ **NARRATOR:** The week continues in this way: the days start early, the family works hard together, the children attend school. Each day brings new work to be done; delicious, fresh, home-cooked meals to prepare and eat; and pleasant evenings of games, sewing, and stories. Even Kim gets to be storyteller one night. Quickly, the week passes, and Kim must say goodbye.

> ✳ **FLUENCY TIP**
>
> When you see a colon as in the narrator's part, pause a little longer than you would at a comma.

Readers' Theater 8, SV 9781419031731

DAD: *(at home)* So tell me, how was your trip?

KIM: My trip was amazing! The Yoders welcomed me and taught me so much. You didn't tell me that Amish culture was so multi-faceted. I thought they were just people who worked in agriculture and wore pilgrim-type costumes to be nonconformists. Dad, everything they do, they do with pride and precision. We could learn some valuable lessons from the Amish.

DAD: Sounds like you already did. Hey, I hate to interrupt this, but I need to go pick up your brother.

KIM: Great, I want to tell him the highlights of my trip and teach him how to play marbles. I also want to tell him a story I heard during my visit.

DAD: *(surprised)* OK, then. That sounds great.

KIM: I'll set the table for supper and tidy up a bit—you know, do my part. *(She pulls a homemade purple apron from her suitcase and ties it around her waist. She beams at her father.)*

DAD: *(big smile)* That would be wonderful, Kimmy.

Readers' Theater 8; SV 9781419031731

Comprehension

Write your answer to each question on the lines below.

1. Why do you think Kim is upset when she learns she is going to stay on a farm?
   _____

2. Why does Kim visit the Amish? _____
   _____

3. Describe the Amish school with as many details as you can recall. _____
   _____

4. Do you agree that car ownership divides the wealthy from the poor? Why or why not?
   _____

5. Name five ways Amish life is different from Kim's life. _____
   _____

6. What do you think Kim will do differently after her visit? _____
   _____

7. What do you think of the Amish way of life? What do you see as the benefits?
   Disadvantages? _____
   _____

8. If eighth grade were your last year of school, how would that affect your future? How
   would you feel about leaving school after eighth grade? _____
   _____

9. Imagine living like the Amish. What would be most difficult for you? Most enjoyable?
   _____
   _____

10. What activities do you enjoy that do not require electricity or other modern
    conveniences? _____
    _____

Vocabulary

Write the vocabulary word that answers each question.

philosophy	corrupt	conform	culture
incessantly	reproach	consumerism	

1. What word means the same as the lifestyle of a group of people in a certain place? _____

2. What do people who always follow the rules do? _____

3. What word means a set of beliefs? _____

4. What word is a synonym for *scold*? _____

5. What do you call buying a lot of things? _____

Extension

1. With a partner or in a small group, discuss the following.

   • Name one activity you could do in your community that would help others.

   • If you had no homework and no electricity, what would you do in the evenings?

   • What three things could you do around the house that would be helpful to your family?

2. In a small group, discuss the effect of TV commercials on consumerism.

   • What products are you asked to buy and why?

   • How do the commercials make you feel?

   • Do you think commercials are beneficial or detrimental to our society? Why?

Answer Key

Chemical Reactions

Comprehension, page 30

(Suggested responses)

1. The materials used in the first experiment are a bottle with a narrow neck, vinegar, baking soda, a funnel, a straw, water, and a balloon. The materials used in the second experiment are baking soda, vinegar, a small zipper bag, warm water, a tissue, and a measuring cup. The materials used in the third experiment are light corn syrup, glycerin, water, vegetable oil, yellow food coloring, blue food coloring, glasses, a funnel, and a large glass jar. The vinegar, baking soda, water, and funnel are used more than once. Also, the students wear safety goggles, gloves, and aprons for the experiments.
2. The baking soda and vinegar create an acid-base reaction that makes carbon dioxide gas.
3. Ian's gloves turn green because he spills yellow and blue food coloring on them. Red and yellow make orange. Red and blue make purple.
4. Ian has done the experiment before, so he knows what to do.
5. Safety equipment protects scientists in case of accidents.
6. Responses will vary.
7. Responses will vary.
8. Responses will vary.
9. An experiment involves tests to find the answer to a question.
10. Sinda made a hypothesis when she said she thought the water should be layered first.

Vocabulary, page 31

1. experiment
2. procedure
3. synthesize
4. density
5. patent
6. Nobel Prize

What's Green and . . . ?

Comprehension, page 49

(Suggested responses)

1. Dissecting frogs is a way to learn about anatomy.
2. Three parts of a frog's digestive system are the esophagus, the stomach, and the small intestine.
3. Both have a gallbladder, liver, and pancreas.
4. A frog's heart has three chambers, and a human heart has four. A frog has fixed eyelids, and human beings have eyelids that open and close.
5. Responses will vary.
6. Liu is serious and wants to get her work done, while Cary keeps fooling around.
7. Yes, it will bleed because it has red and white blood cells.
8. Responses will vary.
9. Responses will vary.
10. Responses will vary.

Vocabulary, page 50

Answers from top to bottom should read as follows:
7, 1, 3, 6, 2, 4, 5

Something Is Mushrooming!

Comprehension, page 68

(Suggested responses)

1. Rob composts yard trimmings, foodstuff, and shredded newspaper.
2. Trees contribute by taking in carbon dioxide and placing it in the soil, providing protection from winds, and providing shade.
3. You can turn the compost pile over so that it gets more oxygen.
4. Environmental awareness (composting, planting trees, recycling) mushrooms in the neighborhood because of the projects started by the new neighbors.
5. Responses will vary.
6. Lina may suggest that they start a compost pile and recycle more things.
7. Responses will vary.
8. Responses will vary.
9. Responses will vary.
10. Responses will vary.

Vocabulary, page 69

1. vermicomposting
2. environmentalist
3. emissions
4. humus
5. nonpoint-source pollution

The Technology Experiment
Comprehension, page 87
(Suggested responses)

1. The students agree to give up microwave ovens, computers, and clock radios.
2. The experiment lasts one week.
3. Responses will vary.
4. The experiment is most likely intended to show the students how much they depend on electronic devices or how helpful these devices are.
5. Families probably wouldn't go along with the experiment if it meant giving up things like lights.
6. Responses will vary.
7. Wang probably has the hardest time because it takes her so much longer to write her paper.
8. Responses will vary.
9. Responses will vary.
10. Responses will vary.

Vocabulary, page 88

1. experiment
2. minimum
3. lyrics
4. volunteer
5. pertinent

Cities Around the World
Comprehension, page 106
(Suggested responses)

1. He doesn't know what the teens look like, and they don't know him.
2. Kate worries that she's not ready for such a big adventure, that she doesn't know the language, and that she is so far away from home.
3. Kate sees unique insects, a cloud forest, and a volcano.
4. Kate benefits from her trip by learning a new language, learning about different cultures, and making new friends.
5. Responses will vary.
6. Responses will vary.
7. I can infer that the rest of the country is not crowded.
8. Responses will vary.
9. Responses will vary.
10. Responses will vary.

Vocabulary, page 107
Answers from top to bottom should read as follows:
7, 3, 1, 6, 4, 2, 5

The Simple Life
Comprehension, page 125
(Suggested responses)

1. Kim probably thinks staying on a farm will be boring.
2. Kim's parents are going on a business trip, and she is going to stay with relatives who are Amish.
3. Responses will vary.
4. Responses will vary.
5. The Amish don't have TV, telephones, Internet, dishwashers, or air conditioners.
6. Responses will vary.
7. Responses will vary.
8. Responses will vary.
9. Responses will vary.
10. Responses will vary.

Vocabulary, page 126

1. culture
2. conform
3. philosophy
4. reproach
5. consumerism

Answer Key
Readers' Theater 8, SV 9781419031731